Hand-arm vibration

The Control of Vibration at Work
Regulations 2005

Guidance on Regulations

HSE Books

This guidance is issued by the Health and Safety Executive. Following the
guidance is not compulsory and you are free to take other action. But if you do
follow the guidance you will normally be doing enough to comply with the law.
Health and safety inspectors seek to secure compliance with the law and may refer
to this guidance as illustrating good practice.

Contents

Introduction

1   Hand-arm vibration (HAV) is a widespread hazard for employees in many industries and occupations. HAV exposure at work can arise from the use of hand-held power tools (such as grinders or hammer drills), hand-guided machinery (such as lawnmowers and plate compactors) and hand-fed machines (such as pedestal grinders). Prolonged and regular exposure to this vibration can affect the operator's health. But the risks from vibration can be controlled and employees can be protected from ill health caused by vibration. To protect employees, and to comply with the Vibration Regulations, employers need to assess the risks from vibration and plan how to control them.

2   This book contains in-depth guidance on the Control of Vibration at Work Regulations 2005 (the Vibration Regulations) as they relate to hand-arm vibration. It replaces HSG88, the previous Health and Safety Executive (HSE) guidance book on hand-arm vibration, first published in 1994 (ISBN 0 7176 0743 7). It does not contain guidance on those parts of the Regulations which apply only to whole-body vibration as this will be provided in a separate book (L141 ISBN 0 7176 6126 1) due to be published in late 2005.[1] The parts of the Regulations which apply specifically to whole-body vibration are identified by grey shading.

3   General health and safety regulations, supported by HSE guidance, have required employers to control the risks from vibration and protect their employees since the early 1990s, however, the Vibration Regulations now place specific duties on employers. They are based on a European Union Directive* requiring similar basic laws throughout the Union on reducing the risks of vibration-related diseases. If employers comply with the Vibration Regulations and follow HSE's guidance, it will be possible to stop employees developing advanced stages of these diseases. The requirements are straightforward and will not be difficult for employers to carry out.

4   The legal duties described in this book are in addition to the general obligations to safeguard workers' health (including the effects of vibration) which employers have had since 1975 under the Health and Safety at Work etc Act 1974 (the HSW Act). These general obligations also apply to the safeguarding of the health of people who are not employees, such as students, voluntary workers, visitors and members of the public. Employees also have duties under the HSW Act to take care for their own health and safety and that of others whom their work may affect; and to co-operate with employers so that they may comply with health and safety law.

5   This book is divided into colour-coded parts to help readers go directly to the information that is most relevant to them. Other useful information is in a series of appendices.

Part 1 Legal duties of employers to control the risks to health and safety from hand-arm vibration

6   Part 1 of the book includes the text of the Vibration Regulations and explains what they mean and what they require you to do. It sets out your legal obligations as an employer to control risks to health and safety from exposure to hand-arm vibration (HAV), including preventing HAV-related diseases such as damage to the tissues of the hands and arms, which cause the conditions known as hand-arm vibration syndrome (HAVS) and vibration-related carpal tunnel syndrome. This part will also be of interest to health and safety professionals.

---

* Council Directive 2002/44 /EC of 6 July 2002 on the minimum health and safety requirements regarding the risks arising from physical agents (vibration).

Parts 2-5 Practical guidance for employers

7   Parts 2-5 include practical information for employers on carrying out risk assessment, estimating vibration exposure, controlling risks, arranging health surveillance, understanding the duties of machinery manufacturers and suppliers to their customers, and how to obtain competent help with your assessment and control of risks.

Part 6 Technical guidance for health and safety advisors and specialists
Part 7 Guidance for occupational health professionals on health surveillance

8   Parts 6 and 7 of the book provide supplementary technical and medical guidance for health and safety professionals, specialists and occupational health professionals. Most employers will probably not need to read these parts, although some information may be relevant if they are planning to do some of the work themselves, for example the base level annual health surveillance. Readers of Parts 6 and 7 will also find it helpful to familiarise themselves with Parts 1 to 5 so that they have a good understanding of what the employer has to do and what help they need.

9   HSE has also produced a free leaflet and quick-reference pocket card about the new requirements. For employers, leaflet INDG175(rev2) *Control the risks from hand-arm vibration*[2] includes a brief introduction to the Vibration Regulations and provides the essential information that you will need to be able to comply with them. The pocket card INDG296(rev1) *Hand-arm vibration: Advice for employees*[3] contains straightforward advice for employees. Both can be obtained from HSE Books (see 'Further information' at the back of the book for details) or downloaded from HSE's vibration website at www.hse.gov.uk/vibration.

PART 1: LEGAL DUTIES OF EMPLOYERS TO CONTROL THE RISKS TO HEALTH AND SAFETY FROM HAND-ARM VIBRATION

Regulation 1

Citation and commencement

Regulation 1

These Regulations may be cited as the Control of Vibration at Work Regulations 2005 and shall come into force on 6th July 2005.

Regulation 2

Interpretation

Regulation

(1) In these Regulations -

"daily exposure" means the quantity of mechanical vibration to which a worker is exposed during a working day, normalised to an 8-hour reference period, which takes account of the magnitude and duration of the vibration;

"emergency services" include -

(a) police, fire, rescue and ambulance services;

(b) Her Majesty's Coastguard;

"enforcing authority" means the Executive or local authority, determined in accordance with the provisions of the Health and Safety (Enforcing Authority) Regulations 1998;[a]

"exposure action value" means the level of daily exposure set out in regulation 4 for any worker which, if reached or exceeded, requires specified action to be taken to reduce risk;

"exposure limit value" means the level of daily exposure set out in regulation 4 for any worker which must not be exceeded, save as set out in regulation 6(5);

"the Executive" means the Health and Safety Executive;

"hand-arm vibration" means mechanical vibration which is transmitted into the hands and arms during a work activity;

"health surveillance" means assessment of the state of health of an employee, as related to exposure to vibration;

"mechanical vibration" means vibration occurring in a piece of machinery or equipment or in a vehicle as a result of its operation;

"risk assessment" means the assessment of risk required by regulation 5;

"whole-body vibration" means mechanical vibration which is transmitted into the body, when seated or standing, through the supporting surface, during a work activity or as described in regulation 5(3)(f); and

2

(a) SI 1998/494, as amended by SI 1999/2024, SI 1999/3232, SI 2002/2675 and SI 2004/3168.

"working day" means a daily working period, irrespective of the time of day when it begins or ends, and of whether it begins or ends on the same calendar day.

(2)   In these Regulations, a reference to an employee being exposed to vibration is a reference to the exposure of that employee to mechanical vibration arising out of or in connection with his work.

Application and transitional provisions

(1)   These Regulations shall have effect with a view to protecting persons against risk to their health and safety arising from exposure to vibration at work.

(2)   Subject to paragraph (3), regulation 6(4) shall not apply until 6th July 2010 where work equipment is used which –

(a)   was first provided to employees prior to 6th July 2007 by any employer; and

(b)   does not permit compliance with the exposure limit values,

but in using such equipment the employer shall take into account the latest technical advances and the organisational measures taken in accordance with regulation 6(2).

(3)   For the agriculture and forestry sectors, regulation 6(4) shall not apply to whole-body vibration until 6th July 2014 in respect of work equipment which –

(a)   was first provided to employees prior to 6th July 2007 by any employer; and

(b)   does not permit compliance with the exposure limit value for whole-body vibration

but in using such equipment the employer shall take into account the latest technical advances and the organisational measures taken in accordance with regulation 6(2).

(4)   Where a duty is placed by these Regulations on an employer in respect of his employees, he shall, so far as is reasonably practicable, be under a like duty in respect of any other person, whether at work or not, who may be affected by the work carried out by the employer except that the duties of the employer –

(a)   under regulation 7 (health surveillance) shall not extend to persons who are not his employees; and

(b)   under regulation 8 (information, instruction and training) shall not extend to persons who are not his employees, unless those persons are on the premises where the work is being carried out.

(5)   These Regulations shall apply to a self-employed person as they apply to an employer and an employee and as if that self-employed person were both an employer and an employee, except that regulation 7 shall not apply to a self-employed person.

(6)   These Regulations shall not apply to the master or crew of a ship or to the employer of such persons in respect of the normal shipboard activities of a

ship's crew which are carried out solely by the crew under the direction of the master, and for the purposes of this paragraph "ship" includes every description of vessel used in navigation, other than a ship forming part of Her Majesty's Navy.

Purpose

10   The Vibration Regulations are designed to protect against risks to both health and safety from hand-arm vibration, ie the risk of HAVS and carpal tunnel syndrome in those exposed, and situations where vibration may affect the ability to safely handle controls or read indicators, or where it may interfere with the stability or security of structures.

Transitional period

11   Regulation 3(2) defers the application of the exposure limit value (ELV) (see regulations 4(1) and 6(4)) until 6 July 2010 while it is not reasonably practicable to comply with it, if you are using equipment which was already in use before 6 July 2007.

12   The transitional period applies only to the exposure limit value. The other requirements of the Regulations come into force from 6 July 2005 and must be complied with from that date.

13   The purpose of the transitional period is:

(a)   to allow a reasonable period of time for you to introduce new working methods, designs of equipment etc, which eliminate or reduce vibration exposure;

(b)   to allow time for equipment with reduced vibration emission to be developed and introduced.

14   Exposures above the exposure limit value arising from use of any equipment supplied to workers before 6 July 2007 (ie your own existing equipment, or second-hand equipment, or equipment from hire companies) may continue right up to 6 July 2010, but only if it is not reasonably practicable to purchase or hire newer, lower-vibration tools or to introduce alternative working methods which would reduce exposures below the exposure limit value. You will need to keep the availability of lower-vibration equipment or work methods under regular review. If it becomes reasonably practicable for you to introduce lower-vibration equipment or work methods before 6 July 2010, then you must do so.

15   It is important to remember that the transitional period is not a licence to do nothing at all. Even if you cannot reduce exposures below the exposure limit value you must reduce them to as low a level as is reasonably practicable (see regulation 6(2)) and plan your longer-term strategy for getting exposures below the limit value by July 2010. Any equipment first brought into use after July 2007, whether bought or hired, will need to be used in a way that will keep vibration exposure below the exposure limit value. So you will need to choose and manage the use of such equipment carefully to ensure the exposure limit value is not exceeded.

16   The following two examples may help you decide if use of the transitional period would be appropriate to your work activities.

Example 1

In 2005, a company uses a concrete breaker and a disc cutter purchased in 2000 for work which exposes one of their employees to around 7-8 m/s² $A(8)$ each day (ie above the new exposure limit value of 5 m/s² $A(8)$). They consider what could be done to reduce exposure below the exposure limit value and decide that no suitable tools with lower vibration are, at that time, available nor is there any suitable alternative method for getting the work done without using the tools. However, they conclude that the time spent by the employee using the breaker can be reduced by introducing job rotation and making use of an excavator-mounted breaker for some of the work. This action reduces the daily exposure to around 6 m/s² $A(8)$. This exposure remains above the exposure limit value but given that there is nothing else it is reasonably practicable to do to reduce it further, the company decides it is able to continue to use the tools in this way at least until 2010 because of the transitional period.

However, in 2008, the company identifies a new lower-vibration breaker that has just come onto the market which would help reduce the daily exposure of the worker to 3 m/s² $A(8)$. The new breaker proves in trials to be suitable and effective for the work they do. The old model had been used for eight years and had a potential life of a further 12 years but the cost of replacing it early was not regarded as grossly disproportionate. In these circumstances the company can no longer justify continued use of the old breaker under the transitional period arrangements. They purchase the lower-vibration breaker and are able to comply with the exposure limit value from this date (2008).

Example 2

A quarrying company uses state-of-the-art rock drills which expose their employees to around 9 m/s² $A(8)$ (ie above the new exposure limit value of 5 m/s² $A(8)$). The introduction of job rotation allows them to reduce exposure time resulting in daily exposures of 6 m/s² $A(8)$. Although this exposure exceeds the exposure limit value, the company is not able to find an alternative method to do the work and is able to continue to use the equipment until the transitional period ends in 2010. The transitional period allows them some time to develop an alternative way of working.

People who are not your employees

17   Sometimes your activities may cause employees of other employers, or non-employees, to be exposed to vibration, for example where sub-contractors use vibrating equipment for work you specify and control, or where volunteers are engaged alongside workers. Regulation 3(4) applies to all the employers involved and each will have a responsibility:

(a)   to their own employees; and

(b)   so far as is reasonably practicable, to anyone else who is exposed to vibration in work activities under their control.

18   This responsibility applies to all the duties under these Regulations except health surveillance (regulation 7) for anyone other than their own employees, while information, instruction and training (regulation 8) need only be given to the employees of others in relation to the specific job they are undertaking for you.

19   Employers will need to exchange information and collaborate when working on joint projects to ensure they fulfil their duties without confusion or unnecessary duplication. On multi-contractor sites they will usually need to agree on who is to co-ordinate action to comply with health and safety requirements; this will normally be the person in overall control of the work. Where contractors and sub-contractors are involved it is usually best for responsibilities to be set out in the contractual arrangements. For construction projects, the principal contractor under the Construction (Design and Management) Regulations 1994 (as amended)[4] should ensure co-operation between all contractors through the use of pre-tender health and safety plans, method statements etc.

The self-employed

20   Regulation 3(5) defines both employer and employee to include self-employed people. So if you are self-employed you will need to take action as set out in the Vibration Regulations to protect yourself from vibration risks. Although self-employed people are not required to provide themselves with health surveillance in accordance with regulation 7, it is nevertheless recommended that they follow the guidance in Part 5 'Health surveillance for HAVS' and, where appropriate, consult an occupational health service provider. This will ensure that HAVS symptoms are identified and will allow risk controls to be reviewed and revised as necessary.

Trainees

21   The Health and Safety (Training for Employment) Regulations 1990[5] require trainees on relevant work training schemes in the workplace (but not those on courses at educational establishments such as universities or schools) to be treated as the employee of the person whose undertaking is providing the training. Your duties towards trainees will include all the requirements of these Regulations including assessment and control of risks, provision of health surveillance, provision of information and training and consideration of whether any trainees might be at particular risk.

Application to ships, other vessels and aircraft

22   The Control of Vibration at Work Regulations 2005 apply to work taking place in ships, boats, and other vessels operated by Her Majesty's Navy and to work on any vessel carried out alongside shore workers when it is moored or in dock. Regulation 3(6) states that these Regulations do not apply to the master and crew of a ship. This refers to work done by the crew under the control of the ship's master when the ship is under way or work done by them in harbour when no shore-based workers are involved. However, in the future, similar regulations relating to control of vibration on merchant shipping and fishing vessels, enforced by the Maritime and Coastguard Agency, will apply to all vessels in UK waters and to UK-registered vessels in international waters.

23   The Vibration Regulations apply to aircraft in flight over British soil. However, the Regulations are not intended to interfere with the flight safety of aircraft. Any proposals to alter an aircraft to comply with the Regulations should be agreed with the Civil Aviation Authority (CAA).

Exposure limit values and action values

(1)   For hand-arm vibration –

(a)   the daily exposure limit value is 5 m/s² A(8);

(b)   the daily exposure action value is 2.5 m/s² A(8),

and daily exposure shall be ascertained on the basis set out in Schedule 1 Part I.

(2)   For whole-body vibration –

(a)   the daily exposure limit value is 1.15 m/s²A(8);

(b)   the daily exposure action value is 0.5 m/s²A(8),

and daily exposure shall be ascertained on the basis set out in Schedule 2 Part I.

24   The daily exposure limit value (ELV) is the maximum amount of vibration an employee may be exposed to on any single day (see regulation 6(4)). The daily exposure action value (EAV) is the level of daily exposure to vibration above which you are required to take certain actions to reduce exposure (see regulations 6(2), 7(1)(b) and 8(1)(b)).

25   Guidance on how to determine employees' daily exposure for comparison with the exposure values is given in Part 2.

Assessment of the risk to health created by vibration at the workplace

(1)   An employer who carries out work which is liable to expose any of his employees to risk from vibration shall make a suitable and sufficient assessment of the risk created by that work to the health and safety of those employees and the risk assessment shall identify the measures that need to be taken to meet the requirements of these Regulations.

(2)   In conducting the risk assessment, the employer shall assess daily exposure to vibration by means of –

(a)   observation of specific working practices;

(b)   reference to relevant information on the probable magnitude of the vibration corresponding to the equipment used in the particular working conditions; and

(c)   if necessary, measurement of the magnitude of vibration to which his employees are liable to be exposed,

and the employer shall assess whether any employees are likely to be exposed to vibration at or above an exposure action value or above an exposure limit value.

(3)   The risk assessment shall include consideration of –

(a)   the magnitude, type and duration of exposure, including any exposure to intermittent vibration or repeated shocks;

(b)   the effects of exposure to vibration on employees whose health is at particular risk from such exposure;

(c)   any effects of vibration on the workplace and work equipment, including the proper handling of controls, the reading of indicators, the stability of structures and the security of joints;

(d)   any information provided by the manufacturers of work equipment;

(e)   the availability of replacement equipment designed to reduce exposure to vibration;

(f)   any extension of exposure at the workplace to whole-body vibration beyond normal working hours, including exposure in rest facilities supervised by the employer;

(g)   specific working conditions such as low temperatures; and

(h)   appropriate information obtained from health surveillance including, where possible, published information.

(4)   The risk assessment shall be reviewed regularly, and forthwith if –

(a)   there is reason to suspect that the risk assessment is no longer valid; or

(b)   there has been a significant change in the work to which the assessment relates,

and where, as a result of the review, changes to the risk assessment are required, those changes shall be made.

(5)   The employer shall record –

(a)   the significant findings of the risk assessment as soon as is practicable after the risk assessment is made or changed; and

(b)   the measures which he has taken and which he intends to take to meet the requirements of regulations 6 and 8.

Risk assessment

26   The purpose of the assessment is to enable you to make a valid decision about the measures necessary to prevent or adequately control the exposure of your employees to HAV. It enables you to demonstrate readily to others who may have an interest, eg employees, safety representatives and enforcement authorities that you have from the earliest opportunity considered:

(a)   all the factors related to the risk;

(b)   the practicability of preventing exposure;

(c)   the steps which need to be taken to achieve and maintain adequate control of exposure where prevention is not reasonably practicable;

(d)   the need for health surveillance;

(e)   how and when to put the steps you have decided on into action.

27   See Part 2 for more detailed guidance on risk assessment. Paragraphs 28-47 explain what the various terms mean in regulation 5 (italicised and in inverted commas) and their effects on the risk assessment.

"A suitable and sufficient assessment"

28   An assessment will be suitable and sufficient if it identifies:

(a)   where there may be a risk from HAV;

(b)   a soundly based estimate of your employees' exposures and a comparison with the exposure action value and exposure limit value;

(c)   the available risk controls;

(d)   the identification of those individuals who may be more at risk;

(e)   the steps you plan to take to control and monitor those risks;

(f)   a record of the assessment.

29   Your exposure estimate will only be soundly based if it uses data which can be judged to be reasonably representative of your work process or, where you have made measurements, they have been done competently. In most cases where the assessment evidence suggests that exposure is unlikely to exceed the exposure action value it is sufficient to record that fact, though you are still required to reduce exposure to as low a level as reasonably practicable. Some employees, eg those with existing health problems, may be at risk from exposures below the exposure action value and need to be protected by additional control measures. If exposure is likely to be above the exposure action value, a more systematic assessment may be required. Alternatively, you may decide to use the broad benchmarks of exposure provided in HSE guidance and say this in your risk assessment (see Part 2 for further advice).

"The measures that need to be taken to meet the requirements of these Regulations"

30   When you have identified the work processes which expose your employees to vibration you should decide what can be done to eliminate or reduce the risks, and when to take action. If the exposure action value is likely to be exceeded you must establish a programme of formal risk-control measures (regulation 6(2)) including a timetable for action. Further guidance on what to do is given in paragraphs 31-47 and in Parts 2 and 3.

"Observation of specific working practices"

31   To assess the daily exposure to vibration of a worker (or a group of workers doing similar work) it is necessary to know:

(a)   which tasks expose employees to vibration;

(b)   which employees are exposed;

(c)   what equipment they use;

(d)   what they use it for; and

(e)   the total time they are in contact with the equipment while it is operating.

32   These details can be obtained by observing the employee. The person need not be observed for a complete day, but for a period or periods long enough to provide a representative sample of a typical or average day's exposure to vibration. Observation of the work will generally produce a much more accurate indication of equipment usage time than asking the employee to make an estimate. Work patterns also need careful consideration. For example some workers may only use vibrating tools for certain periods in a day or week. Typical usage patterns should be established as these will be an important factor in calculating a person's likely vibration exposure. Parts 2 and 6 give more details of how to carry out observation of working practices.

"Relevant information on the probable magnitude of the vibration"

33   To be relevant, the vibration information you use to do your vibration assessment needs to match as closely as possible the likely vibration performance of the equipment you plan to use in the way you plan to use it. There are several possible sources of suitable information on vibration levels. These include:

(a)   vibration emission values declared in the equipment handbook;

(b)   additional information from the equipment supplier;

(c)   internet databases;

(d)   research organisations;

(e)   vibration consultancies;

(f)   HSE's website;

(g)   trade associations;

(h)   measurements made in your own workplace.

34   However, it is important to check that the vibration data is reasonably representative of your equipment as used in your work activities. Guidance on how to check the suitability of vibration emission data is in Parts 2 and 4.

"If necessary, measurement of the magnitude of vibration"

35   This makes clear that measurement may sometimes be required, but that it may not be necessary if suitable vibration data are available. If your estimate leaves you uncertain about whether vibration exposures are likely to be above or below the exposure action value, you could simply assume that the exposure action value is exceeded and proceed with your programme of control measures and health surveillance (see regulations 6, 7 and 8). If you decide to arrange for measurements to be taken, it may be possible to collaborate with others, eg your trade association, to share the costs of obtaining relevant vibration exposure data.

36   You may also need to arrange for measurements to be done when you require confirmation that your control actions have reduced exposure, particularly if you need to show that you have brought them below the exposure limit value. However, as long as you can clearly demonstrate that you have introduced effective controls so far as is reasonably practicable which, based on suitable available vibration data, can reasonably be expected to keep exposures below the exposure limit value, it may not be necessary to measure.

37 Measurement of vibration requires specific competency, including training in how to use specialised measuring equipment, and a good understanding of these Regulations and the factors which can lead to inaccurate and misleading measurement. You could arrange for you or one of your staff to undergo training in HAV measurement and assessment, or you could employ a contractor with suitable qualifications and/or experience and an understanding of these Regulations (see 'How to obtain competent advice and assistance' in Part 3 paragraphs 192-196) to do the measurement and, if necessary, produce a risk assessment and control programme.

"Magnitude, type and duration of exposure"

38 The factors which govern a person's daily vibration exposure are the magnitude (level) of vibration and the length of time the person is exposed to it. The greater the magnitude and/or the longer the duration of exposure, the greater the person's vibration exposure will be. Other characteristics of the vibration, such as the frequency, may also affect the risk. These are dependent on how the equipment operates, eg hammer action tools and rotary action tools have very different vibration characteristics. The pattern of work may also be relevant, eg intermittent exposures may indicate a lower risk than a long, uninterrupted exposure.

"Employees whose health is at particular risk"

39 Under regulation 6(6) the measures to be taken must be adapted to take into account employees who are particularly sensitive to vibration. These include:

(a) employees with existing HAVS or other diseases of the hands, arms, wrists or shoulders;

(b) employees with diseases affecting blood circulation, eg diabetes, or nerve disorders affecting the hands or arms, eg carpal tunnel syndrome.

40 More comprehensive information about the factors affecting sensitivity is in Part 7 which contains guidance for occupational health professionals.

"Any effects of vibration on the workplace and work equipment"

41 Vibration from work equipment can cause damage to other workplace equipment or structures which may create safety risks, eg the risk of materials or equipment falling from overhead platforms or joints moving apart. Vibration may also affect people's ability to read instruments or indicators or to handle controls. You should identify any such risks and take action to control them.

"Information provided by the manufacturers of work equipment"

42 You should ask the suppliers of equipment known to vibrate in use for information on the vibration emission of their product and how any residual risks should be managed. Manufacturers of machinery are required by the Supply of Machinery (Safety) Regulations 1992 (as amended)[6] to design and construct their products to minimise vibration risks and to provide their customers with information on vibration emissions from their equipment, on safe use of the equipment and to warn of residual risks. Part 4 provides more detail on the legal duties of equipment manufacturers, importers and suppliers and on the interpretation of the information provided.

Guidance

"The availability of replacement equipment designed to reduce exposure to vibration"

43   For many types of equipment there will be models available with reduced vibration emission, eg chainsaws with anti-vibration suspended handles. When buying, hiring or replacing equipment you should take these factors into account so far as is reasonably practicable. However, it is also important to select equipment that is suitable for the work you are going to do and this may not be the one with the lowest vibration emission. Your equipment supplier(s) should be able to advise you. You should regularly review the tools in use to check if there are any suitable new reduced-vibration tools which would reduce the vibration exposure for a particular operation/task. It will help your long-term management of work equipment if you introduce a clearly defined purchasing policy for selection of suitable lower-vibration equipment.

5(3)(e)

Guidance

"Specific working conditions such as low temperatures"

44   Working in cold and/or wet conditions will tend to trigger attacks of vibration white finger in people who have the disease (see paragraphs 225-229). You should make sure that employees work in these conditions only when unavoidable and that they are provided with suitable protective clothing which will allow them to keep warm and dry.

5(3)(g)

Guidance

"Appropriate information obtained from health surveillance"

45   If you already have a health surveillance programme for HAVS the results (anonymised and grouped to protect medical-in-confidence information about individual workers) should indicate whether new cases of vibration-related disease have appeared or whether existing cases have worsened. This should help you to decide whether the risk is being controlled effectively or whether you need to do more to control it. Published research which includes the effects on the health of workers who have used vibrating equipment similar to that used by your employees may also help you to assess the risk.

5(3)(h)

Guidance

"The risk assessment shall be reviewed regularly"

46   The risk assessment should be reviewed when you identify any changes in availability or suitability of equipment or in work processes likely to offer reduced vibration exposure, or if you have any doubt about the effectiveness of the controls implemented. In any case, you should review your risk assessment at least every three years, but you may wish to review it sooner if:

(a)   the level of risk is high;

(b)   there is doubt that your control measures remain effective;

(c)   there is the likelihood of better work methods or equipment becoming available.

5(4)

Guidance

"Record . . . the significant findings of the risk assessment"

47   Your record of the risk assessment can be kept in any convenient form. The record must contain information on the significant findings of the assessment and the measures taken (or planned). The record should include:

(a)   the tasks assessed;

(b)   the risk of HAVS for your employees;

5(5)

(c) the likelihood of the exposure action and limit values being exceeded;

(d) the measures you have put in place to control and manage the risk;

(e) a programme of measures with timescales, for any future controls you plan to introduce;

(f) the appropriate information, instruction and training to be provided to employees;

(g) the scheme of health surveillance in use or planned.

Regulation 6

Elimination or control of exposure to vibration at the workplace

(1) The employer shall ensure that risk from the exposure of his employees to vibration is either eliminated at source or, where this is not reasonably practicable, reduced to as low a level as is reasonably practicable.

(2) Where it is not reasonably practicable to eliminate risk at source pursuant to paragraph (1) and an exposure action value is likely to be reached or exceeded, the employer shall reduce exposure to as low a level as is reasonably practicable by establishing and implementing a programme of organisational and technical measures which is appropriate to the activity.

(3) The measures taken by the employer in compliance with paragraphs (1) and (2) shall be based on the general principles of prevention set out in Schedule 1 to the Management of Health and Safety at Work Regulations 1999[(a)] and shall include consideration of –

(a) other working methods which eliminate or reduce exposure to vibration;

(b) choice of work equipment of appropriate ergonomic design which, taking account of the work to be done, produces the least possible vibration;

(c) the provision of auxiliary equipment which reduces the risk of injuries caused by vibration;

(d) appropriate maintenance programmes for work equipment, the workplace and workplace systems;

(e) the design and layout of workplaces, work stations and rest facilities;

(f) suitable and sufficient information and training for employees, such that work equipment may be used correctly and safely, in order to minimise their exposure to vibration;

(g) limitation of the duration and magnitude of exposure to vibration;

(h) appropriate work schedules with adequate rest periods; and

6

(a) SI 1999/3242, as amended by SI 2003/2457.

(i)   the provision of clothing to protect employees from cold and damp.

(4)   Subject to regulation 3(2) and (3) and paragraph (5), the employer shall –

(a)   ensure that his employees are not exposed to vibration above an exposure limit value; or

(b)   if an exposure limit value is exceeded, he shall forthwith –

(i)   reduce exposure to vibration to below the limit value;

(ii)   identify the reason for that limit being exceeded; and

(iii)   modify the measures taken in accordance with paragraphs (1) and (2) to prevent it being exceeded again.

(5)   Paragraph (4) shall not apply where the exposure of an employee to vibration is usually below the exposure action value but varies markedly from time to time and may occasionally exceed the exposure limit value, provided that –

(a)   any exposure to vibration averaged over one week is less than the exposure limit value;

(b)   there is evidence to show that the risk from the actual pattern of exposure is less than the corresponding risk from constant exposure at the exposure limit value;

(c)   risk is reduced to as low a level as is reasonably practicable, taking into account the special circumstances; and

(d)   the employees concerned are subject to increased health surveillance, where such surveillance is appropriate within the meaning of regulation 7(2),

and exposure within the meaning of this paragraph shall be ascertained on the basis set out in Schedule 1 Part II for hand-arm vibration and Schedule 2 Part II for whole-body vibration.

(6)   The employer shall adapt any measure taken in compliance with the requirements of this regulation to take account of any employee or group of employees whose health is likely to be particularly at risk from vibration.

Control of exposure

48   This regulation means you have to take action to eliminate the risks from vibration exposure completely wherever it is reasonably practicable to do so (regulation 6(1)). Paragraphs 50-68 explain what some of the terms in regulation 6 mean. You will need to consider whether there are alternative processes, better equipment and/or better working methods which would largely eliminate these risks.

49   If it is not reasonably practicable to eliminate the risks completely, you should reduce them to as low a level as is reasonably practicable (regulation 6(1)). It is important to note that exposures below the exposure action value are not risk free, so action should not stop at this level of exposure if further reductions can be achieved at a reasonable cost. You should:

(a)   introduce a formal programme of control measures whenever an employee's daily exposure to vibration is likely to exceed the exposure action value (regulation 6(2)) (see paragraphs 50-63 and Parts 2 and 3);

(b)　not expose anyone above the exposure limit value (regulation 6(4)) (see paragraphs 64-65).

"Establishing and implementing a programme of organisational and technical measures"

50　The action plan produced during your vibration risk assessment should describe a programme of control measures and your plans to put it into action with realistic timescales. Such a programme is required when your vibration assessment shows that any of your employees are likely to be exposed above the exposure action value.

51　The programme of control measures should be devised to reduce the risks from vibration exposure to as low a level as is reasonably practicable. The actions you take will depend on the particular work activities and processes and the possibilities for control. Detailed guidance on selecting and introducing suitable controls is in Part 3.

52　Some controls may take time to put in place, particularly where equipment must be replaced or new industrial processes developed. The programme should also state clearly which managers, supervisors and employees have responsibility for delivering the various parts of the programme and by when. It should also include provisions for testing the effectiveness of control measures.

"The general principles of prevention"

53　Schedule 1 of the Management of Health and Safety at Work Regulations 1999[7] lists the general principles of prevention:

(a)　avoiding risks;

(b)　evaluating the risks which cannot be avoided;

(c)　combating the risks at source;

(d)　adapting the work to the individual, especially regarding the design of workplaces, the choice of work equipment and the choice of working and production methods, with a view, in particular, to alleviating monotonous work and work at a predetermined work-rate and to reducing their effect on health;

(e)　adapting to technical progress;

(f)　replacing the dangerous by the non-dangerous or the less dangerous;

(g)　developing a coherent overall prevention policy which covers technology, organisation of work, working conditions, social relationships and the influence of factors relating to the working environment;

(h)　giving collective protective measures priority over individual protective measures; and

(i)　giving appropriate instructions to employees.

54　The list of possible control measures in regulation 6(3) is specific to vibration but follows similar principles.

Guidance

6(3)(a)

Guidance

6(3)(b)

Guidance

6(3)(c)

Guidance

6(3)(d)

Guidance

6(3)(e)

Guidance
6(3)(f)

Guidance

6(3)(g)

"Other working methods which eliminate or reduce exposure"

55   Other methods of work which can eliminate or reduce exposure to vibration include automation or mechanisation of work previously done with hand-operated or hand-fed machines. For example, a hand-operated pneumatic road breaker might be replaced in some work activities by a hydraulic pick mounted on an excavator arm, or a stand-mounted tamper when compacting sand-filled moulds, rather than a hand-held tamper.

"Choice of work equipment of appropriate ergonomic design"

56   The choice of work equipment can be an important means of reducing exposure to vibration. Some newer designs of power tool can emit significantly lower levels of vibration than traditional types as well as being easy to use, eg lighter weight and ergonomically designed to avoid strain on the user's hands and arms. However, the equipment selected must be suitable for the job and the efficiency of the tool should be taken into account when evaluating the likely reduction in exposure from changing a tool.

"The provision of auxiliary equipment"

57   Auxiliary equipment which can affect the risk of vibration injuries includes consumables for power tools such as balanced grinding wheels, drills and chisels. The manufacturer can usually advise on selection of the correct equipment for the job. Any equipment which modifies a machine, such as an 'anti-vibration handle' produced by a third party, should not be used unless its use is endorsed by the machine manufacturer.

"Appropriate maintenance programmes"

58   Maintenance of machinery, undertaken in accordance with the manufacturer's recommendations, should prevent unnecessarily high vibration emissions resulting from worn parts, loose components etc. Operators should be instructed to report any unusually high vibration levels and to sharpen or replace consumables (grinding wheels, drills, chisels etc) when necessary.

"The design and layout of workplaces"

59   The design and layout of the workplace can affect the risks associated with vibration exposure. If your employees have to grip the tool tightly, apply large feed forces or support the weight of a heavy machine, they are likely to increase the vibration energy absorbed by the hands. Ergonomic principles in the design of the tools and their installation in the workplace (eg enabling neutral postures for tool operators or using balancers to support the weight of heavy grinders) can improve working conditions and productivity as well as reducing vibration risks.

"Suitable and sufficient information and training for employees"

60   See regulation 8 for guidance on information and training for employees.

"Limitation of the duration and magnitude of exposure"

61   When all reasonably practicable steps have been taken to reduce the vibration magnitude, the final resort for compliance with the exposure limit value is to limit the duration of exposure. The exposure points systems described in Part 2 (paragraphs 133-134), can be a useful management tool for this purpose. Also see Part 3 for more details.

"Appropriate work schedules with adequate rest periods"

62   The scientific basis for recommending appropriate work schedules and breaks from vibration is incomplete. However, it is good practice to schedule short periods of exposure with frequent breaks rather than have long uninterrupted vibration exposures.

"Protect employees from cold and damp"

63   Ensure your employees are able to keep warm and dry as this will help to maintain good blood circulation and reduce the likelihood of vascular symptoms (finger blanching).

"Ensure . . . employees are not exposed . . . above the exposure limit value"

64   You must not permit an employee to be exposed above the exposure limit value. Your programme of measures must be designed to prevent this level of exposure. If you find that the exposure limit value is being exceeded, you must immediately take action to reduce exposure and identify the reason for the overexposure.

65   You should not consider reduction below the exposure limit value to be a target – you must reduce exposure as low as you reasonably can, and below the exposure action value if this is reasonably practicable (risks are still significant for exposures between the two values and some people will still be at risk if exposed at the action value). This may mean reducing the time for which the employee uses the equipment each day, eg spreading that particular task over several days or sharing it between two or more employees. See paragraphs 11-16 for information on the transitional period for the exposure limit value.

"Exposure averaged over one week"

66   Weekly averaging of daily exposure allows for occasional daily exposures above the exposure limit value. However, there are stringent conditions for its use. Regulations 6(1) and 6(2) still apply and it will often be reasonably practicable to spread the exposure over more than one day to keep each day's exposure below the exposure limit value. Also, to qualify for weekly averaging, exposures must be usually (ie on most days) below the exposure action value. Where weekly averaging is used, you should also increase the health surveillance of employees. Weekly averaging is most likely to apply in cases of emergency work, eg involving the rescue services or intensive urgent work using chainsaws to clear fallen trees following a storm etc.

67   The weekly averaging scheme would permit a maximum exposure on any one day of 11 m/s^2 $A(8)$ when exposure on the remaining days of the week is zero, or 10 m/s^2 $A(8)$ when exposure on each of the other four days of the week is just below 2.5 m/s^2 $A(8)$ – the exposure action value.

"Employees . . . likely to be particularly at risk from vibration"

68   Paragraph 39 describes the employees in this category. You will need to make special efforts to restrict exposure for such individuals, and an increased level of health surveillance may also be appropriate.

Health surveillance

(1) If –

(a) the risk assessment indicates that there is a risk to the health of his employees who are, or are liable to be, exposed to vibration; or

(b) employees are likely to be exposed to vibration at or above an exposure action value,

the employer shall ensure that such employees are placed under suitable health surveillance, where such surveillance is appropriate within the meaning of paragraph (2).

(2) Health surveillance, which shall be intended to prevent or diagnose any health effect linked with exposure to vibration, shall be appropriate where the exposure of the employee to vibration is such that –

(a) a link can be established between that exposure and an identifiable disease or adverse health effect;

(b) it is probable that the disease or effect may occur under the particular conditions of his work; and

(c) there are valid techniques for detecting the disease or effect.

(3) The employer shall ensure that a health record in respect of each of his employees who undergoes health surveillance in accordance with paragraph (1) is made and maintained and that the record or a copy thereof is kept available in a suitable form.

(4) The employer shall –

(a) on reasonable notice being given, allow an employee access to his personal health record; and

(b) provide the enforcing authority with copies of such health records as it may require.

(5) Where, as a result of health surveillance, an employee is found to have an identifiable disease or adverse health effect which is considered by a doctor or other occupational health professional to be the result of exposure to vibration the employer of that employee shall –

(a) ensure that a suitably qualified person informs the employee accordingly and provides the employee with information and advice regarding further health surveillance, including any health surveillance which he should undergo following the end of the exposure;

(b) ensure that he is himself informed of any significant findings from the employee's health surveillance, taking into account any medical confidentiality;

(c) review the risk assessment;

(d) review any measure taken to comply with regulation 6, taking into account any advice given by a doctor or occupational health professional or by the enforcing authority;

(e) consider assigning the employee to alternative work where there is no risk from further exposure to vibration, taking into account any advice given by a doctor or occupational health professional; and

(f) provide for a review of the health of any other employee who has been similarly exposed, including a medical examination where such an examination is recommended by a doctor or occupational health professional or by the enforcing authority.

(6) An employee to whom this regulation applies shall, when required by his employer and at the cost of his employer, present himself during his working hours for such health surveillance procedures as may be required for the purposes of paragraph (1).

"Suitable health surveillance"

69   Health surveillance is a programme of systematic health checks to identify early signs and symptoms of disease and to allow action to be taken to prevent its progression. It is also useful in monitoring the effectiveness of your controls. This regulation requires employers to introduce suitable health surveillance for those of their employees who are at risk from exposure to HAV. Detailed guidance on suitable health surveillance for HAVS is in Part 5.

"Where such surveillance is appropriate"

70   Health surveillance must be provided not only for employees likely to be exposed above the exposure action value but also for others whom the risk assessment identifies may be at risk, eg employees who are particularly sensitive to vibration (see paragraph 39). Health surveillance is not appropriate for individuals whose daily exposures exceed the exposure action value only on rare occasions and where the risk assessment identifies that the risk of ill health is consequently very low.

"Health records"

71   These records will contain information on the outcome of the health surveillance and information on the individual's fitness to continue to work with vibration exposure. They should not contain confidential medical information, which should be kept in the medical record held by the occupational health professional.

Action required when health surveillance reveals that any employees have suffered ill health as a result of exposure to vibration

72   The doctor who has made the diagnosis should explain the significance of the results to the employee and give advice on the risks of continuing with vibration exposure.

73   The doctor or occupational health professional should inform you of the findings of health surveillance procedures, in particular whether or not the employee is fit to continue work involving exposure to vibration. However, they will not disclose medical-in-confidence information to you without the written consent of the employee.

74   You should prevent further harm to the individual by acting on any advice from the doctor or occupational health professional and, where necessary, removing the employee from exposure to HAV. You should review your vibration

risk assessment to decide whether to take action to protect the rest of the workforce. Where other workers have similarly been exposed to HAV you should arrange for them to be placed under health surveillance.

75 Anonymised health surveillance results for groups of employees should help you monitor how well your vibration risk control programme is working. Such information should be suitably adapted to protect individuals' identities and be made available to safety or employee representatives.

Attendance for health surveillance

76 Regulation 7(6) requires your employees to co-operate with your health surveillance programme by attending their health surveillance appointments. However, you must arrange for this in normal working hours and cover any costs (eg lost earnings, travel). You should consult with your trade union safety representative, or employee representative and the employees concerned before introducing health surveillance. It is important that your employees understand that the aim of health surveillance is to protect them from developing advanced symptoms of ill health so that their ability to continue to work is not affected. You will need their understanding and co-operation if health surveillance is to be effective. It may be appropriate to include details of health surveillance requirements in your employees' contracts of employment.

Information, instruction and training

(1) If –

(a) the risk assessment indicates that there is a risk to the health of his employees who are, or who are liable to be, exposed to vibration; or

(b) employees are likely to be exposed to vibration at or above an exposure action value,

the employer shall provide those employees and their representatives with suitable and sufficient information, instruction and training.

(2) Without prejudice to the generality of paragraph (1), the information, instruction and training provided under that paragraph shall include –

(a) the organisational and technical measures taken in order to comply with the requirements of regulation 6;

(b) the exposure limit values and action values set out in regulation 4;

(c) the significant findings of the risk assessment, including any measurements taken, with an explanation of those findings;

(d) why and how to detect and report signs of injury;

(e) entitlement to appropriate health surveillance under regulation 7 and its purposes;

(f) safe working practices to minimise exposure to vibration; and

(g) the collective results of any health surveillance undertaken in accordance with regulation 7 in a form calculated to prevent those results from being identified as relating to a particular person.

(3)   The information, instruction and training required by paragraph (1) shall be updated to take account of significant changes in the type of work carried out or the working methods used by the employer.

(4)   The employer shall ensure that any person, whether or not his employee, who carries out work in connection with the employer's duties under these Regulations has suitable and sufficient information, instruction and training.

Information, instruction and training for employees

77   You should be informative and open to your exposed workers and to their safety and employee representatives on the results of your risk assessment. Employees should be properly trained to carry out their jobs safely. Regulation 8(2) lists some of the issues that must be covered, but it is not exhaustive.

78   Employers should ensure employees fully understand the level of risk they may be exposed to, how it is caused and the possible health effects, ie:

(a)   which work equipment and processes cause vibration risks and their respective levels of risk;

(b)   how their personal daily exposures compare with the exposure action and limit values;

(c)   what symptoms of ill health they should look out for, to whom they should report them and how they should report them;

(d)   what control measures you plan to introduce to reduce risks;

(e)   the use of personal protective equipment where required, eg the need to keep warm;

(f)   what training you plan for operators, supervisors and managers in their respective roles to ensure control of exposure, eg through correct selection, use and maintenance of equipment or restriction of exposure times;

(g)   what health surveillance will be provided, how you are going to provide it and why it is important, as well as the overall findings (in anonymous form);

(h)   what employees' duties are to:

(i)   follow instructions they are given on safe working practices;

(ii)   report problems with their equipment such as unusually high vibration levels; and

(iii)   co-operate with your programme of control measures and health surveillance.

79   You can provide the information, instruction and training in different ways, including:

(a)   presentations;

(b)   computer-based training;

(c)   individual counselling and training;

(d)   leaflets and posters;

(e)   videos;

(f)   short local training sessions.

80   No single way will be suitable for all circumstances and you will need to reinforce the messages from time to time, eg by giving 'tool-box' talks. You should draw employees' attention to any relevant advice provided by HSE, trade associations etc and provide them with the HSE pocket card (INDG296(rev1)).

81   You should make sure that you give the information in a way in which the employee can be expected to understand (eg you might need to make special arrangements if the employee is not fluent in English or cannot read).

82   Working with trade-union-appointed safety representatives or other employee representatives can be a very useful means of communicating and reinforcing health and safety matters in your workplace. You are required by the Safety Representatives and Safety Committees Regulations 1977[8] and the Offshore Installations (Safety Representatives and Safety Committees) Regulations 1989[9] to make certain information available to safety representatives appointed under the Regulations. The representatives are entitled to see some of your documents which will normally include your vibration assessment and action plan covering those employees represented. You should make sure the representatives know how the information can be obtained and give them any necessary explanation of their meaning. There is also a duty on you to provide information to employee representatives elected under the Health and Safety (Consultation with Employees) Regulations 1996[10] which apply to groups of workers who are not covered by a trade-union-appointed safety representative.

Information, instruction and training in connection with the employer's duties

83   Anyone who helps you to comply with your duties under these Regulations (for example by making vibration measurements, determining exposures or planning for control of risk through changes to industrial processes or working practices) must have suitable and sufficient information, instruction and training. This means that they must be competent to undertake this responsibility.

84   Part 3 (paragraphs 192-196) contains guidance on appropriate levels of knowledge and expertise for competent assessment and management of hand-arm vibration. Whether you employ a consultant or use members of your staff for these purposes you should ensure that they have the necessary understanding and experience.

Exemption certificates for emergency services

(1)   Subject to paragraph (2), the Executive may, by a certificate in writing, exempt any person or class of persons from regulation 6(4) in respect of activities carried out by emergency services which conflict with the requirements of that paragraph, and any such exemption may be granted subject to conditions and to a limit of time and may be revoked by a certificate in writing at any time.

(2)   The Executive shall not grant any such exemption unless it is satisfied that the health and safety of the employees concerned is ensured as far as possible in the light of the objectives of these Regulations.

85   Any emergency service wishing to seek exemption under this regulation should contact HSE for further advice. HSE is likely only to consider applications made in relation to an emergency service as a whole rather than from local units. Emergency services will only need to apply for exemption after the end of the transitional period on 6 July 2010.

Regulation 10

Exemption certificates for air transport

Regulation

(1)   Subject to paragraph (2), the Executive may, by a certificate in writing, exempt any person or class of persons from regulation 6(4) in respect of whole-body vibration in the case of air transport, where the latest technical advances and the characteristics of the workplace do not permit compliance with the exposure limit value despite the technical and organisational measures taken, and any such exemption may be granted subject to conditions and to a limit of time and may be revoked by a certificate in writing at any time.

(2)   The Executive shall not grant any such exemption unless –

(a)   it consults the employers and the employees or their representatives concerned;

(b)   the resulting risks are reduced to as low a level as is reasonably practicable; and

(c)   the employees concerned are subject to increased health surveillance, where such surveillance is appropriate within the meaning of regulation 7(2).

10

Regulation 11

Exemptions relating to the Ministry of Defence

Regulation

(1)   Subject to paragraph (2), the Secretary of State for Defence may, by a certificate in writing, exempt any person or class of persons from regulation 6(4) in respect of activities carried out in the interests of national security which conflict with the requirements of that paragraph, and any such exemption may be granted subject to conditions and to a limit of time and may be revoked by a certificate in writing at any time.

(2)   The Secretary of State shall not grant any such exemption unless he is satisfied that the health and safety of the employees concerned is ensured as far as possible in the light of the objectives of these Regulations.

11

Regulation 12

Extension outside Great Britain

Regulation

These Regulations shall apply to and in relation to any activity outside Great Britain to which sections 1 to 59 and 80 to 82 of the 1974 Act apply by virtue of the Health and Safety at Work etc. Act 1974 (Application outside Great Britain) Order 2001[(a)] as those provisions apply within Great Britain.

12

(a) SI 2001/2127.

86   These Regulations apply to all work activities on offshore installations, wells, pipelines and pipelines works and to certain connected activities within the territorial waters of Great Britain or in designated areas of the UK Continental Shelf. They also apply to certain other activities within territorial waters, including the construction and operation of wind farms.

Amendments

(1)   In the Offshore Installations and Wells (Design and Construction etc.) Regulations 1996,[a] paragraph 67 of Schedule 1 shall be omitted.

(2)   In the Provision and Use of Work Equipment Regulations 1998,[b] to the end of the list in regulation 12(5) add –

"(g) the Control of Vibration at Work Regulations 2005".

(a) SI 1996/913, amended by SI 1997/1993.
(b) SI 1998/2306.

Hand-arm vibration

Regulations 4(1) and 6(5)

87   This Schedule provides definitions of hand-arm vibration exposure relevant to the exposure action and limit values set out in the Regulations. The Schedule is not generally intended to be used by employers, who should be able to assess daily vibration exposure adequately by following the guidance in this book.

Part I: Daily exposure to vibration

The daily exposure to vibration (A(8)) of a person is ascertained using the formula:

$$A(8) = a_{\mathrm{hv}} \sqrt{\frac{T}{T_0}}$$

where:

a_{hv} is the vibration magnitude, in metres per second squared (m/s²);

T is the duration of exposure to the vibration magnitude a_{hv}; and

T_0 is the reference duration of 8 hours (28,800 seconds).

To avoid confusion between vibration magnitude and daily exposure to vibration, it is conventional to express daily exposure to vibration in m/s² $A(8)$.

The vibration magnitude, a_{hv}, is ascertained using the formula:

$$a_{\mathrm{hv}} = \sqrt{a_{\mathrm{hwx}}^2 + a_{\mathrm{hwy}}^2 + a_{\mathrm{hwz}}^2}$$

where:

a_{hwx}, a_{hwy} and a_{hwz} are the root-mean-square acceleration magnitudes, in m/s², measured in three orthogonal directions, x, y and z, at the vibrating surface in contact with the hand, and frequency-weighted using the weighting W_{h}.

The definition for the frequency weighting W_{h} is given in British Standard BS EN ISO 5349-1:2001.

Where both hands are exposed to vibration, the greater of the two magnitudes a_{hv} is used to ascertain the daily exposure.

If the work is such that the total daily exposure consists of two or more operations with different vibration magnitudes, the daily exposure ($A(8)$) for the combination of operations is ascertained using the formula:

$$A(8) = \sqrt{\frac{1}{T_0} \sum_{i=1}^{n} a_{\mathrm{hv}i}^2 \, T_i}$$

where:

n is the number of individual operations within the working day;

$a_{\mathrm{hv}i}$ is the vibration magnitude for operation i; and

T_i is the duration of operation i.

Part II: Exposure to vibration averaged over one week

The exposure to vibration averaged over one week ($A(8)_{\text{week}}$) is the total exposure occurring within a period of seven consecutive days, normalised to a reference duration of five 8-hour days (40 hours). It is ascertained using the formula:

$$A(8)_{\text{week}} = \sqrt{\frac{1}{5} \sum_{j=1}^{7} A(8)_j^2}$$

where:

$A(8)_j$ is the daily exposure for day j.

The exposure to vibration averaged over one week is for use only for the purposes of regulation 6(5).

Schedule 2

Whole-body vibration

Regulations 4(2) and 6(5)

Part I: Daily exposure to vibration

The daily exposure to vibration ($A(8)$) of a person is ascertained using the formula:

$$A(8) = ka_w \sqrt{\frac{T}{T_0}}$$

where:

a_w is the vibration magnitude (root-mean-square frequency-weighted acceleration magnitude) in one of the three orthogonal directions, x, y and z, at the supporting surface;

T is the duration of exposure to the vibration magnitude a_w;

T_0 is the reference duration of 8 hours (28,800 seconds); and

k is a multiplying factor.

To avoid confusion between vibration magnitude and daily exposure to vibration, it is conventional to express daily exposure to vibration in m/s^2 $A(8)$.

Daily exposure to vibration ($A(8)$) is evaluated separately for the x, y and z directions of vibration.

For horizontal vibration (x and y directions), $k = 1.4$ and a_w is obtained using the W_d frequency weighting. For vertical vibration (z direction), $k = 1.0$ and a_w is obtained using the W_k frequency weighting.

Definitions for the frequency weightings are given in International Standard ISO 2631-1:1997.

If the work is such that the total daily exposure consists of two or more operations with different vibration magnitudes, the daily exposure ($A(8)$) for the combination of operations is ascertained using the formula:

$$A(8) = \sqrt{\frac{1}{T_0} \sum_{i=1}^{n} a_{wi}^2 T_i}$$

where:

n is the number of individual operations within the working day;

a_{wi} is the vibration magnitude for operation i; and

T_i is the duration of operation i.

Part II: Exposure to vibration averaged over one week

The exposure to vibration averaged over one week ($A(8)_{week}$) is the total exposure occurring within a period of seven consecutive days, normalised to a reference duration of five 8-hour days (40 hours). It is ascertained using the formula:

$$A(8)_{week} = \sqrt{\frac{1}{5} \sum_{j=1}^{7} A(8)_j^2}$$

where:

$A(8)_j$ is the daily exposure for day j.

The exposure to vibration averaged over one week is for use only for the purposes of regulation 6(5).

PART 2: ASSESS VIBRATION RISKS AND DEVELOP AN ACTION PLAN FOR CONTROL

- Are my employees at risk from vibration?

- How can I assess the risk?

- How can I estimate the daily vibration exposure?

- How can I plan to manage the risk?

88   This section includes guidance for employers on the assessment of the risks from exposure to vibration. It will help you decide whether HAV represents a risk to your employees and whether you need to take action. It includes guidance on working out vibration exposures, identifying employees whose exposure may exceed the action or limit value, and deciding whether you need a risk control action plan and health surveillance.

89   The Vibration Regulations require that you make a 'suitable and sufficient' assessment of the risks from vibration. This will include:

- identifying employees who may be at risk from exposure to HAV;

- a soundly based estimate of your employees' vibration exposures compared with the exposure action value and exposure limit value;

- the available and appropriate options for controlling risk;

- the steps you plan to take to control and monitor those risks as required by the Vibration Regulations (regulations 6, 7 and 8); and

- a record of:

   ❑   the assessment;

   ❑   the person(s) responsible for the assessment;

   ❑   the control measures you have taken and their effectiveness; and

   ❑   your plans for further action.

Five steps to vibration risk assessment

90   There are five basic steps in assessing the risks from HAV at work:

Step 1   Look to see whether you have a vibration problem to manage, ie whether HAV is likely to be a significant hazard in your workplace (see paragraphs 91-102).

Step 2   Identify all workers likely to be exposed (see paragraphs 103-104).

Step 3   Evaluate the risks arising from the vibration – estimate daily vibration exposures and identify appropriate further actions to control the risk and comply with regulations 6, 7 and 8 (see paragraphs 105-145).

Step 4   Record your findings (see paragraphs 146-148).

Step 5   Review the assessment and revise it as required (see paragraphs 149-152).

Step 1: Do I have a problem to manage?

91   It is your duty as an employer to establish if your employees are likely to be at risk from HAV and, if so, to assess and manage the risk. This initial exercise, however, can be a straightforward process and may not require specialist knowledge of vibration. A starting point is to consider the industry you work in, the processes involved and the tools and equipment used, and answer some basic questions.

Do you use hand-held, hand-guided or hand-fed powered equipment in your business?

92   If you use such work equipment, you should identify employees who may be at risk from vibration and you may need to take action to control the risk.

93   In some industries, such as those listed in Table 1, the work processes and the tools and equipment used are known to be associated with vibration-related disease. If your business is in one of these industry sectors, some of your employees are likely to be at risk. However, any high-vibration tools or processes, **particularly if they cause tingling or numbness in the hands during or after use**, can present a risk, and use of percussive (hammer-action) tools is believed to be particularly hazardous. Your equipment suppliers should inform you if the use of their tools carries a risk from vibration (see Part 4 'Information from manufacturers and suppliers of machinery').

Table 1 Some industries and processes associated with HAV

Vibration is a common hazard in many industry sectors, including:

- general and heavy engineering, fabrication and metalworking;

- forestry;

- estate management (eg maintenance of grounds, parks, watercourses, road and railway verges);

- foundries;

- shipbuilding and ship repair;

- construction and civil engineering;

- road and railway construction and maintenance;

- mines and quarries;

- manufacture of concrete products;

- motor vehicle manufacture and repair;

- utilities (gas, electricity, water, telecommunications etc).

High-risk processes include:

- drilling and breaking rock, concrete, and other materials;

- consolidating or compacting sand, concrete or aggregate;

- riveting, caulking, hammering, clinching, flanging and hammer swaging;

- preparing and dressing welds;

- surface preparation, including scabbling, de-scaling and paint removal;

- grinding, sanding or polishing wood, metal, stone, rubber, plastics and ceramics;

- cutting metal, wood, grass, stone, bone etc;

- holding or supporting objects being worked upon by machine;

- component or product assembly.

94   The Reporting of Injuries, Diseases and Dangerous Occurrences Regulations 1995 (RIDDOR) require employers to report to the enforcing authority any diagnosed cases of hand-arm vibration syndrome (HAVS) arising from certain work activities.[11] If your business involves any of these activities (see the list in Appendix 1), all of which are known to be associated with HAVS, you should assume you have a potential problem with vibration and that a programme of control measures and health surveillance may be required.

Do you use impact or percussive (eg hammer-action) tools?

95   With impact or percussive tools you will usually need to take control action. You should certainly be taking action if individual employees are operating them for more than about fifteen minutes per day unless you have evidence that the exposure is not enough to exceed the exposure action value.

96   The hammer action tools with the highest vibration emissions can exceed the exposure action value in less than five minutes.

Do you use rotary action machines (eg grinders, sanders)?

97   Non-percussive tools and machines (eg rotary action tools) generally have lower levels of vibration than percussive tools. However, many still require action to control risks. You should certainly be taking action if individual employees are operating them for more than about one hour per day unless you have evidence that the exposure is not enough to exceed the exposure action value.

98   The rotary action tools with the highest vibration emissions can exceed the exposure action value within about fifteen minutes.

Do manufacturers or suppliers of tools or equipment warn of a risk from vibration?

99   If you are using power tools or other machines which could present a risk from vibration, the manufacturer should tell you about it in the handbook. You

should then check that the equipment is suitable for the job and ensure you have appropriate controls in place to manage the risk. If the equipment manufacturer has supplied information on the likely vibration emission for work similar to yours, this will help you estimate the levels of exposure of your operators. (More guidance to help you interpret suppliers' information is in Part 4 'Information from manufacturers and suppliers of machinery').

Have any employees been affected by vibration?

100 HAVS and 'vibration white finger' are now generally well-known conditions in some industries (as well as carpal tunnel syndrome, a disorder of the hand and arm), and some of your employees may already be aware of the symptoms to look out for. If not, talk to your workforce, or their representatives, and their supervisors, tell them about HAVS and encourage them to report any problems. These symptoms include:

■   numbness and tingling in the fingers;

■   not being able to feel things properly, which makes it difficult to work with small objects or do everyday tasks such as fastening buttons;

■   fingers going white (blanching) and becoming red and painful on recovery (particularly in the cold and wet). This is sometimes known as 'vibration white finger', 'dead finger' or 'dead hand'. During these attacks the fingers feel numb;

■   joint pain and stiffness in the hand and arm and reduced grip strength.

101 If any of your vibration-exposed employees already have symptoms of HAVS, this shows that you may need to take action, although in the absence of reported symptoms there may still be a risk to be managed, which should be identified in your risk assessment.

102 The health surveillance section (see Part 5) explains how to make arrangements for pre-exposure assessment and on-going health surveillance of your workforce. This, together with any self-reporting, should identify employees with symptoms and enable diagnosis of HAVS. In such cases, you will need to take appropriate action to control or eliminate further vibration exposures. You should also start or continue health surveillance of your employees to check in the long term that your controls are effective.

Summary: Do I have a problem to manage?

If the answer to one or more of the following questions is **yes** then you should assume your employees are at risk from vibration and take steps to reduce their exposure and the risk by following the guidance in this book.

■   Do you use rotary action power tools or machines for more than about an hour per day?

■   Do you use hammer action power tools for more than about 15 minutes per day?

■   Do you work in an industry where HAVS is known to be a problem?

■   Do you work with any of the industrial processes for which HAVS is reportable?

> - Do any of your equipment suppliers warn of a vibration risk?
>
> - Do any of your employees have symptoms of HAVS?

Step 2: Identify the people at risk

103 For hand-arm vibration, identifying employees at risk is usually a simple procedure. The employees likely to be harmed are those exposed to the vibration, ie those who operate the vibrating tools and equipment you have identified. This includes those employees who spend most of the day working with vibrating machinery, those who may use power tools regularly, but for short periods, such as fitters and maintenance staff, and those whose vibration exposure may vary widely from day to day, such as some construction workers.

104 Different people may have different levels of vibration exposure. There is a significant risk that a worker will develop HAVS if he or she is exposed regularly above the exposure action value. The Vibration Regulations require you to do all that is reasonably practicable to reduce such exposures. However, exposures at levels below the action value are not 'safe' and you must still do what you can to avoid or reduce the risk.

Step 3: Evaluate the risks and plan for control

105 Steps 1 and 2 should help you decide whether your employees are at risk from HAV. If you think there is a risk to be managed, you need to consider the likely levels of exposure to vibration and develop a suitable action plan.

What is the purpose of an exposure assessment?

106 The purpose of the assessment is to:

- identify where there is a risk to employees, so that you can produce an action plan for controlling exposure and managing the risk in accordance with the Vibration Regulations;

- determine your employees' daily vibration exposures, with enough accuracy to establish who is likely to be exposed at or above the exposure action value or the exposure limit value;

- identify any additional information which might be needed for the action plan, including how the work processes or work equipment can be replaced or modified to control vibration exposures, whether any special training is required, who should receive health surveillance and how it will be provided.

What other information is needed to assess risk?

107 You need to assess the risk, not just the daily exposure. The Vibration Regulations require you to consider employees whose health is at particular risk from vibration, the working conditions, particularly the temperature in the workplace, and the type of vibration exposure (see paragraphs 38 and 44).

108 If any of your employees are particularly likely to be affected by exposure to vibration you should take this into account when planning to control the risk. If any of your vibration-exposed employees have HAVS, other diseases of the hands, arms, wrists or shoulders (eg carpal tunnel syndrome), diseases affecting blood circulation (eg diabetes) or certain other disorders you should take advice from an occupational health service provider on individual employees' fitness to work with the vibration exposure.

109 The Vibration Regulations also require you to consider the 'type' of vibration exposure in addition to the level of daily exposure. For example, if the daily exposure occurs over several periods with breaks between them, the risk to health may be less than a long period of uninterrupted exposure.

What information is needed to assess daily exposure?

110 To estimate a worker's daily vibration exposure you will need two pieces of information:

- the average magnitude (level) of the vibration at the surface in contact with the hand; and

- the daily exposure time (the time for which an employee's hand is actually in contact with that vibration).

What is the vibration magnitude?

111 Vibration magnitude is the level of vibration at the hand position on the tool, handle, workpiece etc. This is expressed as an acceleration value in metres per second squared (m/s^2).

112 The vibration magnitude for the use of a particular tool or a particular work process can be highly variable. It can be affected by the condition of the tool, the material being worked, the operator's technique and how it was measured. It is usually very difficult to obtain a precise value, so an indication of the average vibration magnitude is needed. Both hands may be exposed to vibration and you should base your assessment on the hand with the greater exposure.

113 The Regulations require you to assess your employees' daily exposures, so you can plan the necessary action to control the risk. It is not important to obtain a precise daily exposure (it will probably vary from day to day anyway). You just need enough information to establish whether it is likely that the exposure action or limit value will be exceeded. You may be able to do this without having to make vibration measurements in your workplace.

114 When you have obtained a vibration magnitude value for each tool or vibrating process, and the corresponding exposure duration for each of them, you can calculate the daily vibration exposure for each employee or job. Some simple methods are described in this section. You should compare the likely daily exposures with the exposure action and limit values. Remember that the daily exposure is an indication of the level of risk to health. If the exposure is likely to exceed the exposure limit value, the risk is high and the Vibration Regulations require you to take immediate action to prevent further exposures above this level. When the exposure is likely to exceed the exposure action value you need to have an action plan to minimise the exposures and control the risk. You also need to provide health surveillance for employees likely to be exposed above the action value.

Where can I get information on vibration magnitude?

115 Manufacturers or suppliers of tools or machines can be an important source of information. They must provide you with information on risks from vibration, and suppliers of portable hand-held and hand-guided machines must also declare a vibration emission value (see Part 4 'Information from manufacturers and suppliers of machinery').

116 Vibration emission values declared by machine manufacturers are measured using standard laboratory-based test codes. Some of these values are obtained in artificial test conditions and may underestimate the vibration likely to be produced in real use. You should ask the supplier for a value (or, more helpfully, a range of values) that represents the likely vibration for the equipment or tool when used in circumstances similar to those in your own workplace (see Part 4).

117 Other possible sources of vibration data include trade associations, government bodies, consultants, technical or scientific publications and on-line databases. At the time of writing (2005), two websites providing free access to a range of manufacturers' standard vibration emission data, and some values measured in real use, are available at:

■   http://www.las-bb.de/karla/index_.htm

■   http://vibration.arbetslivsinstitutet.se/eng/havhome.lasso

118 The vibration information you use to estimate vibration exposures should have been measured on tools or machines similar to yours, and in broadly similar operating conditions. Ideally you will find vibration information for the specific equipment (make and model) you use or plan to use. However, if this is not available, you may need to use data for similar equipment as a starting point, replacing this with more specific information when it becomes available. When identifying vibration data for your assessment, consider the following factors:

■   the type of equipment (eg road breaker, grinder);

■   the power source (eg pneumatic, electric);

■   the class of equipment (eg power rating, operating speed, size or weight);

■   any anti-vibration features (eg suspended handles);

■   the task for which the equipment was used when the vibration was measured (eg breaking concrete, grinding steel);

■   the material being worked;

■   accessories or inserted tools (eg type of chisel or grinding disc).

119 To satisfy yourself of the quality or relevance of available vibration magnitude information, it is good practice to compare data from two or more sources.

120 If you are unable, at least in the short term, to obtain representative vibration data for any of your tools or work activities it may be possible to estimate the magnitude from other sources. Table 2 contains examples of vibration magnitudes that have been measured by HSE on tools in real work situations. HSE expects to make more information of this kind available on its website (www.hse.gov.uk/vibration) in the future.

121 Finally, if you have no available information on the likely in-use vibration magnitude for a hand-held or hand-guided machine, you can make a rough estimate using the tool manufacturer's declared emission value. Because this is likely to be less than the vibration in real use, it is recommended that you apply a scaling factor. Experience has shown that for many tools, doubling the declared value will bring it closer to the vibration magnitudes found in real use. A rough estimate of daily exposure, based on such a value, may be enough to demonstrate the need for you to take action to reduce the exposure and control the risk.

Table 2 Examples of vibration magnitudes measured by HSE on equipment in use at work

Road breakers	Typical	12 m/s^2
	Modern tool designs, good operating conditions and trained operators	5 m/s^2
	Worst tools and operating conditions	20 m/s^2
Demolition hammers	Modern tools	8 m/s^2
	Typical	15 m/s^2
	Worst tools	25 m/s^2
Hammer drills/combi hammers	Typical	9 m/s^2
	Best tools and operating conditions	6 m/s^2
	Worst tools and operating conditions	25 m/s^2
Needle scalers	Modern tool designs	5-7 m/s^2
	Older tool designs	10-25 m/s^2
Scabblers (hammer type)	Typical	20-40 m/s^2
Angle grinders (large)	Modern vibration-reduced designs	4 m/s^2
	Other types	8 m/s^2
Angle grinders (small)	Typical	2-6 m/s^2
Clay spades/jigger picks	Typical	16 m/s^2
Chipping hammers (metal-working, foundries)	Typical fettling	18 m/s^2
	Modern tool designs	10 m/s^2
Pneumatic stone-working hammers	Vibration-reduced hammers and sleeved chisels	8-12 m/s^2
	Older tools, conventional chisels	30 m/s^2
Chainsaws	Typical	6 m/s^2
Brushcutters	Typical	4 m/s^2
	Best	2 m/s^2
Sanders (random orbital)	Typical	7-10 m/s^2

Are vibration measurements required?

122 Although you are not automatically expected to make vibration measurements, the Vibration Regulations do require measurements where it is not otherwise possible to adequately assess the exposure and establish whether the exposure action or limit value is likely to be exceeded. There may be situations when you may need to have vibration measurements made in your workplace, for example:

■ it may not be clear from the limited information available whether the daily exposure is likely to remain below the exposure limit value;

■ you may wish to check the effectiveness of actions taken to control vibration exposure by making 'before and after' measurements;

■ you may be using vibrating equipment for an unusual purpose, of which the manufacturer approves but has limited previous experience and so cannot provide vibration information.

123 You should remember, however, that hand-arm vibration magnitudes can be highly variable, and what is measured on one occasion is only a sample.

124 Vibration measurement can be a difficult and complex task. You may choose to make measurements in-house or employ a specialist for this task. It is important that that whoever makes the measurements is competent (see 'How to obtain competent advice and assistance' paragraphs 192-196).

What is the exposure time?

125 Once you have assessed or measured the vibration magnitude, you will need to identify the time for which an employee is exposed in a day. This is not the overall time spent on the job, but the 'contact time' or 'trigger time' (often much shorter) for which the operator's hands are actually exposed to the vibration.

126 Operators will often overestimate the time they spend in contact with the vibrating tool, machine or hand-held workpiece and you should assess the daily contact time by observing a sample of typical work and considering how much of the time they are actually being exposed to the vibration. The best method of estimating the daily exposure time will depend on the pattern of use of the equipment.

127 For continuous tool operation, such as using a grinder for several hours to remove large amounts of material, or operating a mower for long periods, observe work during a representative part of the working day and record the proportion of the time for which the equipment is operated. A stopwatch or video recording can be used for this.

128 For intermittent tool operation, such as drilling holes in masonry or fettling castings on a pedestal grinder, you may have access to information on the number of repeated operations that occur during the day from the amount of work done (for example, the number of holes drilled or the number of castings fettled). Observe the work over a representative period and work out an average duration for a single operation. Multiply this by the daily number of operations.

What is the daily vibration exposure (A(8) value)?

129 A person's daily vibration exposure is, like the vibration magnitude, expressed in acceleration units of m/s². The daily exposure can be thought of as the average vibration spread over a standard working day of eight hours, adjusted to take account of the actual total exposure time (ie contact time or trigger time). To avoid confusion with vibration magnitudes, it is conventional to add 'A(8)' after the units when quoting a daily vibration exposure, for example: '5 m/s² A(8)'.

130 If the total exposure time happens to be exactly eight hours (unlikely in practice), then the daily vibration exposure has the same value as the average vibration magnitude. For example, if someone is exposed to vibration at 3 m/s² for a total of eight hours in a day, their daily exposure will be 3 m/s² A(8). If the exposure time is less than eight hours (typically the case) their exposure is less than 3 m/s² A(8). If an employee's daily exposure time is more than eight hours (rare in practice, but possible if long shifts are worked) then their exposure is greater than 3 m/s² A(8).

131 Table 3 gives a range of vibration magnitudes, together with the corresponding exposure times, which would result in exposures at the exposure action value (2.5 m/s² A(8)) and the exposure limit value (5 m/s²A(8)).

Vibration magnitude (m/s²)	2.5	3.5	5	7	10	14	20
Time to reach exposure action value (hours)	8	4	2	1	$\frac{1}{2}$	$\frac{1}{4}$	8 min
Time to reach exposure limit value (hours)	>24	16	8	4	2	1	$\frac{1}{2}$

Table 3 Example vibration magnitudes and exposure times required to reach the exposure action value of 2.5 m/s² A(8) and the exposure limit value of 5 m/s² A(8)

132 Figure 1 shows how the vibration magnitude and exposure time are combined to give daily exposures. Exposures that lie in the green area (for example, a magnitude of 3 m/s² and a duration of 2 hours) are below the exposure action value; those in the yellow area are above the exposure action value and those in the red area are above the exposure limit value.

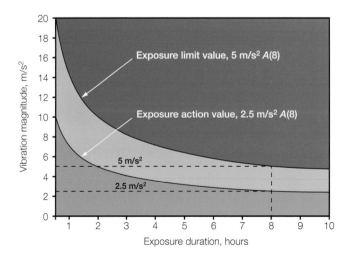

Figure 1 The relationship between vibration magnitude (level), exposure duration and the exposure action and limit values

Exposure points system and ready-reckoner

133 Table 4 is a 'ready-reckoner' for calculating daily vibration exposures using the vibration magnitude and exposure time. The ready-reckoner covers a range of vibration levels up to 40 m/s^2 and a range of exposure times up to ten hours.

134 The exposures for different combinations of vibration magnitude and exposure time are given in exposure points instead of values in m/s^2 $A(8)$. You may find the exposure points easier to work with than the $A(8)$ values:

■ exposure points change simply with time: twice the exposure time, twice the number of points;

■ exposure points can be added together, for example where a worker is exposed to two or more different sources of vibration in a day;

■ the **exposure action value** (2.5 m/s^2 $A(8)$) is equal to **100 points**;

■ the **exposure limit value** (5 m/s^2 $A(8)$) is equal to **400 points**.

Vibration magnitude m/s^2	15 m	30 m	1 h	2 h	3 h	4 h	5 h	6 h	8 h	10 h
40	800									
30	450	900								
25	315	625	1250							
20	200	400	800							
19	180	360	720	1450						
18	160	325	650	1300						
17	145	290	580	1150						
16	130	255	510	1000						
15	115	225	450	900	1350					
14	98	195	390	785	1200					
13	85	170	340	675	1000	1350				
12	72	145	290	575	865	1150	1450			
11	61	120	240	485	725	970	1200	1450		
10	50	100	200	400	600	800	1000	1200		
9	41	81	160	325	485	650	810	970	1300	
8	32	64	130	255	385	510	640	770	1000	1200
7	25	49	98	195	295	390	490	590	785	865
6	18	36	72	145	215	290	360	430	575	720
5.5	15	30	61	120	180	240	305	365	485	605
5	13	25	50	100	150	200	250	300	400	500
4.5	10	20	41	81	120	160	205	245	325	405
4	8	16	32	64	96	130	160	190	255	320
3.5	6	12	25	49	74	98	125	145	195	245
3	5	9	18	36	54	72	90	110	145	180
2.5	3	6	13	25	38	50	63	75	100	125
2	2	4	8	16	24	32	40	48	64	80
1.5	1	2	5	9	14	18	23	27	36	45
1	1	1	2	4	6	8	10	12	16	20

Daily exposure time

Table 4 Ready-reckoner for vibration exposure

Using the ready-reckoner

1 Find the vibration magnitude (level) for the tool or process concerned (or the nearest value) on the grey scale on the left of the table.

2 Find the exposure time (or the nearest value) on the grey scale across the bottom of the table.

3 Find the value in the table that lines up with the magnitude and time. The completed example overleaf shows how it works for a magnitude of 5 m/s^2 and an exposure time of 3 hours: in this case the exposure corresponds to 150 points.

4   Compare the points value with the exposure action and limit values (100 and 400 points respectively). In this example the score of 150 points lies above the exposure action value. The colour of the square containing the exposure points value tells you whether the exposure exceeds, or is likely to exceed, the exposure action or limit value:

Legend:
- Above limit value
- Likely to be above limit value
- Above action value
- Likely to be above action value
- Below action value

Vibration magnitude m/s²	15 m	30 m	1 h	2 h	3 h	4 h	5 h	6 h	8 h	10 h
40	800									
30	450	900								
25	315	625	1250							
20	200	400	800							
19	180	360	720	1450						
18	160	325	650	1300						
17	145	290	580	1150						
16	130	255	510	1000						
15	115	225	450	900	1350					
14	98	195	390	785	1200					
13	85	170	340	675	1000	1350				
12	72	145	290	575	865	1150	1450			
11	61	120	240	485	725	970	1200	1450		
10	50	100	200	400	600	800	1000	1200		
9	41	81	160	325	485	650	810	970	1300	
8	32	64	130	255	385	510	640	770	1000	1200
7	25	49	98	195	295	390	490	590	785	865
6	18	36	72	145	215	290	360	430	575	720
5.5	15	30	61	120	180	240	305	365	485	605
5	13	25	50	100	150	200	250	300	400	500
4.5	10	20	41	81	120	160	205	245	325	405
4	8	16	32	64	96	130	160	190	255	320
3.5	6	12	25	49	74	98	125	145	195	245
3	5	9	18	36	54	72	90	110	145	180
2.5	3	6	13	25	38	50	63	75	100	125
2	2	4	8	16	24	32	40	48	64	80
1.5	1	2	5	9	14	18	23	27	36	45
1	1	1	2	4	6	8	10	12	16	20

Daily exposure time

5   If a worker is exposed to more than one tool or process during the day, repeat steps 1-3 for each one, add the points, and compare the total with the exposure action value (100) and the exposure limit value (400).

Exposure to more than one source of vibration

135 Where a person is exposed to more than one source of vibration (perhaps because they use two or more different tools or processes during the day) this must be calculated separately for each one. This produces two or more partial vibration exposure values which must be combined to give the overall daily exposure value for that employee. These partial exposures can be added together using exposure points.

136 A knowledge of the partial exposures can help you to decide the priorities in your action plan, ie the tools and processes which provide the largest contributions to a person's overall daily exposure are those which should be given the highest priority for control.

Example 3: Use of partial vibration exposure

A construction company produces large concrete structures. Some of its employees use small pneumatic breakers to remove surplus concrete and needle guns for 'scabbling' (roughening concrete surfaces to provide a bonding surface for additional concrete).

The breakers have an average vibration of about 8 m/s² and are operated for about three hours on some days. The needle guns are old models with a vibration level of 15 m/s² and are operated for up to $\frac{1}{2}$ hour per day. When an employee works with the breaker and the needle gun on the same day, the partial exposures for the two operations are:

Breaker (8 m/s² for 3 hours):	385 points
Scabbling (15 m/s² for $\frac{1}{2}$ hour):	225 points
Total vibration exposure:	**610 points**

The company uses this information and includes the following points in its action plan:

- The exposure limit value (400 points) is exceeded and the employee's exposure must be immediately reduced, at least to below the limit value.

- Although the needle gun has a higher vibration level than the breaker, the use of the breaker accounts for the greater proportion of the employee's overall vibration exposure and is a higher priority for urgent attention than the use of the needle gun.

- The partial exposure from use of the breaker is close to 400 exposure points, so it is likely that the exposure limit value will be exceeded by this work alone. The company introduces a job rotation system that restricts daily use of the breaker by any employee to two hours (giving an exposure of about 255 points, which is well below the limit value).

- The exposure from use of the needle gun alone is greater than the exposure action value (100 points) and must also be reduced to the lowest level reasonably practicable. The tool is replaced by a newer needle gun with a vibration emission of about 5 m/s². This gives a partial exposure of only 25 points which (on its own) is below the action value.

- Because employees who use the breaker are still exposed above the action value, a health surveillance scheme is introduced for them.

The on-line vibration exposure calculator

137 HSE's on-line exposure calculator for hand-arm vibration is an alternative to the ready-reckoner for calculating daily exposures quickly and easily. The calculator is shown in Figure 2 and is available in the vibration section of the HSE website at www.hse.gov.uk/vibration. (Note that there are different calculators for hand-arm vibration and whole-body vibration.)

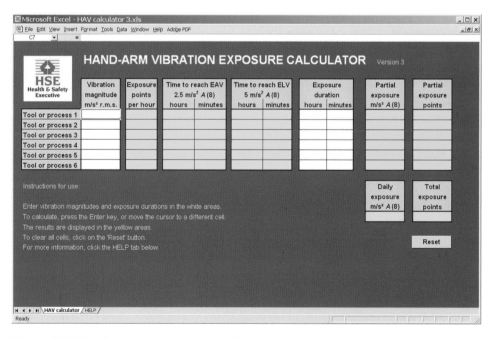

Figure 2 HSE vibration exposure calculator

Using the on-line calculator

1   The calculator may be used online or, if you prefer, you can download and save it on your computer as a spreadsheet file (Microsoft Excel).

2   Click on the white areas and type in a vibration magnitude (in m/s^2) and an exposure duration (in hours and/or minutes). You can do this for up to six different tools or processes.

3   When you have entered all the numbers, press the ENTER key, or click on a different cell. The following values will then be calculated and displayed in the yellow cells on the right.

■   The **Partial exposure** is the vibration exposure (shown in both m/s^2 $A(8)$ and exposure points) for each individual tool or process, and is calculated from the **Vibration magnitude** and the **Exposure duration**.

■   The **Daily exposure**, also in m/s^2 $A(8)$ and exposure points, is calculated from the **Partial exposures**.

4   In addition to the partial and total exposure values, the calculator also uses the vibration magnitudes to produce the following values:

■   **Exposure points per hour**. The number of exposure points for every hour of exposure time for the individual tool or process.

■   **Time to reach EAV** (exposure action value). This is the total exposure time required for the individual tool or process, before the exposure action value (2.5 m/s^2 $A(8)$ or 100 points) is reached.

■   **Time to reach ELV** (exposure limit value). This is the total exposure time required for the individual tool or process, before the exposure limit value (5 m/s^2 $A(8)$ or 400 points) is reached.

5   Figure 3 shows the calculator in use. In this example, an operator uses three tools during a working day. The vibration magnitudes are 2, 6 and 3.5 m/s^2 and the total exposure times are 15, 30 and 90 minutes respectively. These values have been typed into the white cells (you can use hours, minutes or a combination of the two for the exposure duration). The results (in the yellow cells) show the partial exposure values for the three tools and the total exposure which, at 2.2 m/s^2 $A(8)$ or 75 points, is below the exposure action value.

6   The cells can be cleared for another calculation by clicking on the Reset button in the bottom right hand corner.

Note: When you open the spreadsheet you may see a Microsoft Excel message asking you to decide whether to enable or disable macros. If your system settings allow it, you should enable macros. If not, the Reset button will not work. However, the white cells can still be cleared by deleting the contents manually.

HAND-ARM VIBRATION EXPOSURE CALCULATOR Version 3

	Vibration magnitude m/s² r.m.s	Exposure points per hour	Time to reach EAV 2.5 m/s² A (8) hours	minutes	Time to reach ELV 5 m/s² A (8) hours	minutes	Exposure duration hours	minutes	Partial exposure m/s² A (8)	Partial exposure points
Tool or process 1	2	8	12	30	>24			15	0.4	2
Tool or process 2	6	72	1	23	5	33	0.5		1.5	36
Tool or process 3	3.5	25	4	5	16	20	1	30	1.5	37
Tool or process 4										
Tool or process 5										
Tool or process 6										

Instructions for use:

Enter vibration magnitudes and exposure durations in the white areas.
To calculate, press the Enter key, or move the cursor to a different cell.
The results are displayed in the yellow areas.
To clear all cells, click on the Reset button.
For more information, click the HELP tab below.

Daily exposure m/s² A (8)	Total exposure points
2.2	75

Reset

Figure 3 The calculator in use

An action plan to manage the risk

138 While you are assessing the vibration exposures (having identified the work processes which cause them) you should be considering how to eliminate or reduce exposures. The process of risk assessment leads to the identification of reasonably practicable controls and is not complete until you have developed your action plan for risk control.

139 An action plan is an important stage in the risk management/control process, and should include the following:

■ identify the significant sources of vibration;

■ prioritise them as contributors to risk (exposure);

■ identify and evaluate solutions in terms of practicability and cost;

■ plan the introduction of reasonably practicable controls, with timescales;

■ plan the introduction of health surveillance if exposures are still likely to exceed the action value;

■ define management responsibilities and allocate adequate resources to implement controls, evaluate them and monitor progress.

140 The basic methods for reducing vibration exposure and risk, in approximate order of effectiveness, are:

■ eliminate the use of vibrating tools or equipment by introducing mechanisation or alternative, vibration-free processes;

■ reduce vibration exposures by modifying the existing process;

■ replace power tools with suitable modern, efficient, ergonomic, vibration-reduced types through an effective purchasing policy;

■ select appropriate consumables (eg better-balanced and fitted grinding wheels) and replace them when required;

- provide employees with training, information and instruction on safe use of tools and equipment and ensure adequate supervision;

- carry out maintenance of tools and equipment and replace consumables, as recommended by the manufacturer;

- minimise the forces needed to operate and control the tools (eg with tensioners, balancers, jigs, fixtures);

- reduce the exposure time, eg through job rotation.

141 The approach you should take will depend on the availability of reasonably practicable controls, technical advances and the current levels of exposure.

142 For some high-vibration tools there may be no lower-vibration alternatives available, and control through reduction of exposure time may not be reasonably practicable. You should investigate options for the introduction of new processes to eliminate or reduce vibration exposures, particularly if the exposure limit value is exceeded. This may be part of your plans for future capital investment. (In the meantime you must reduce the exposures to the lowest level that is reasonably practicable.)

143 For some high-vibration tools there are lower-vibration alternatives, which may allow you adequately to control the vibration exposure by careful selection and management of the tools you choose.

144 Where the tools produce sufficiently low vibration magnitudes it may be possible to continue to use them, and to control vibration exposures by limiting the daily exposure time and by training your operators to minimise the transmission of vibration to their fingers by correct use of the tools. This will require good supervision and regular review to ensure that the agreed procedures are being observed.

145 Guidance, with examples, on different approaches to the control of risk from HAV can be found in Part 3 'Practical control of vibration exposure and risk'. You must also provide health surveillance for workers whose exposures are likely regularly to exceed the action value, and any others identified in your assessment as being at risk.

Step 4: Record your findings and action plan

146 The Vibration Regulations require that you keep a record of the significant findings of your assessment(s) and what must be done to control the risk. The following checklist is a guide to show the type of information you should include in your assessment records:

- the employees, operations and processes;

- a description of the tools, workpieces, method of working etc;

- any vibration-control measures already in place;

- the likely vibration magnitudes (levels) and sources of this information (manufacturers' information, databases, your own measurements, consultants' advice etc);

- the work patterns and assessments of daily exposure duration;

- people whose daily vibration exposures are likely to exceed the exposure action value and/or the exposure limit value;

- the immediate measures taken to reduce exposure below the exposure limit value, if the assessment shows it is likely to be exceeded;

- identification of where regulations 6, 7 and 8 apply (requirements for reduction of risk and exposure, health surveillance, information and training etc);

- identification of the measures likely to reduce exposure to vibration, and the resources that would be required;

- any further information necessary to help you comply with your duty to reduce exposure and control risk;

- the date of the assessment;

- who made the assessment.

147 If the assessment shows that the daily exposures are low (ie clearly below the exposure action value) then the assessment record should explain this. Remember, however, even if your exposures are below the exposure action value, some employees may still be at risk. The Vibration Regulations require you to eliminate the risk at source or to reduce it to the lowest level reasonably practicable.

148 When exposures are likely to exceed the exposure action value, the assessment should include an action plan showing the priorities for introducing vibration control measures, incorporating:

- immediate actions to control vibration exposure (eg limits on personal daily exposure times);

- planned actions to reduce vibration exposure, such as:

  ❏ alternative production processes that would eliminate or reduce the use of hand-held power tools;

  ❏ obtaining more suitable equipment which would reduce exposures;

  ❏ reduction of vibration transmission to the hands (eg by the use of balancers or tensioners for heavy tools);

- the delivery of information and training, including training on vibration hazards and the correct use of tools (especially vibration-reduced tools);

- arrangements for health surveillance;

- who is responsible (eg managers, supervisors and operators) for carrying out the items of work described in the action plan;

- a timescale and dates for completion of the actions (some actions, particularly the introduction of new work processes, may require investment and development work over several months or years);

- the planned date for review of the assessment;

- any workplace changes, which would require an update of the assessment.

Step 5: Review your assessment

149 You will need to review your assessment whenever there are changes in the workplace which may affect the level of exposure and the risk. Changes that could affect vibration exposures include:

■ the introduction of different machinery or processes;

■ changes in the work pattern or working methods;

■ changes in the number of hours worked with the vibrating equipment;

■ the introduction of new vibration-control measures.

150 The extent of the reassessment will depend on the nature of the changes and the number of people affected by them. A change in hours or work patterns may require a recalculation of the daily exposure for the people affected, but will not necessarily alter the vibration magnitudes. The introduction of new machinery or processes may require a full reassessment.

151 In the longer term, you will also need to review your control measures to ensure they are still relevant and effective. If there is evidence of recent effects on your employees' health, for example, from the results of a health surveillance programme, this would be a clear indication that the actions taken have not been working properly and the risks are not under control.

152 Finally, it is good practice to review your risk assessment and work practices at regular intervals (eg every two or three years) even if nothing obvious has changed. There may be new technology, tool designs or ways of working in your industry which would allow you to reduce risks further.

153 If you follow this guidance correctly, your assessment should be 'suitable and sufficient' and you should be managing the risks in accordance with the Vibration Regulations. However, you may feel you need help with this. See 'How to obtain competent advice and assistance' paragraphs 192-196 for guidance on selecting someone with the necessary knowledge and competence, either from within your own organisation or by employing a consultant.

PART 3: PRACTICAL CONTROL OF VIBRATION EXPOSURE AND RISK

- How can risks from vibration be controlled in practice?

- What can be achieved through the design and management of work processes?

- How can I make sure I have the best equipment for low vibration?

- How can I manage the daily exposure time?

- How can my employees help to control vibration risks?

154 This section gives practical advice on ways to control vibration exposure, starting with elimination of vibration by replacing an industrial process and doing the job a different way. It then includes advice on other ways to reduce the exposure and the risk of ill health, including the selection and use of vibration-reduced equipment and the management of daily exposure time. It includes case studies to help you.

Eliminate vibration exposure in the work processes

155 The most effective and reliable way of eliminating the risk from vibration is to design (or redesign) your work processes so that your employees are not exposed to vibration at all. Where vibration exposures are very high (above the exposure limit value) this approach is sometimes the only way of adequately controlling the vibration risk, and it can often prove cost-effective in the long term. However, re-engineering industrial processes is not always a simple matter. In manufacturing, for example, it can require capital expenditure and effective changes may not happen overnight. In some cases it may be necessary to review your formal standards (such as production methods agreed with customers) to allow these changes to take place.

156 Designers and managers should plan working methods to avoid exposing employees to vibration. It is important to ensure that measures to eliminate vibration exposure do not introduce other significant risks to health or safety.

157 Where effective alternative work methods have been established elsewhere (see boxed examples), you should adopt them if it is reasonably practicable to do so. Your trade association, other industry contacts, equipment suppliers and trade journals may all be able to help you identify good practice in your industry.

158 Your action plan should include systems for ensuring designers and planners are aware of new developments and that they consider alternative designs and methods to:

- avoid (or minimise) the need for operations and equipment exposing workers to vibration;

- introduce vibration-reduced tools or processes;

- improve the ergonomic design of workplaces, equipment, working methods and tasks.

Examples of alternative work processes to eliminate or reduce exposure to vibration

■ In manufacturing, improve component or product design to eliminate fabrication or assembly using hand-held power tools.

■ Change fabrication methods, eg use adhesives, welding, hydraulic squeezing etc to avoid using pneumatic riveting hammers.

■ Replace pneumatic 'buzz' saws with laser profilers for cutting thin steel sheet or removing panels in vehicle bodywork (noting the need to manage any new risks).

■ Specify architectural finishes for building surfaces which avoid the use of needle guns or scabbling tools to produce the required decorative effect.

■ Use prefabricated components to reduce the need for 'cutting and patching' to fit on site.

■ Design metal castings (including selecting the most suitable material and production process) to eliminate or reduce hand finishing (fettling).

■ Mechanise or automate processes that use hand-held, hand-guided or hand-fed machines.

■ Use machine-mounted breakers, mobile road-cutting machines and/or trenching machines instead of hand-operated road breakers for cable laying, water and mains repairs and similar work.

■ De-scale steel structures after fabrication or during repair using abrasive blasting or high-pressure water jetting instead of vibrating pneumatic scaling tools.

■ Split large blocks using hydraulic expanding devices inserted into pre-drilled holes ('bursting').

■ Use milling, turning or other machining operations instead of metal-removing processes using powered hand tools. For example, when fettling castings, it can be more economic, and less hazardous, to rough machine, rather than hand fettle, surfaces which can later be machine finished.

■ Use arc-air and other flame-cutting or gouging methods instead of pneumatic chisels or portable grinders for the rough dressings of castings and similar work.

■ Use preliminary, chemical-polishing processes to cut down on the need for polishing plated components.

Case study 1: Crushing concrete to reduce the use of breakers

The problem During refurbishment of a hospital, it was necessary to demolish a 15 m section of concrete wall. The conventional method, using small pneumatic breakers, would have resulted in vibration exposures of about 12 m/s^2 A(8) and would also have created an unacceptable level of noise in a sensitive environment.

The solution The wall was cut away from the building pillars by drilling overlapping holes (stitch drilling) using a diamond drill. As the drilling machine was held in a clamp, the operators were not exposed to vibration. Each section was then broken up by 'biting' off pieces with a hydraulic concrete crusher. The jaws of this device close slowly, allowing the operators to loosen their grip before crushing takes place.

The cost About 50% more than the cost of using pneumatic breakers.

The result

■ Negligible vibration exposure and very low noise exposure for the operators.

■ Reduced building damage and structure-borne noise as very little vibration is passed into the structure.

■ Reduced dust production.

Figure 4   **Figure 5**

Case courtesy of Specialist Services (Cutting and Drilling) Ltd

159 Revising work processes can sometimes increase productivity. In the ship-building and ship-repair industry, portable grinders and chipping hammers have been used to prepare the edges of plates, to dress welds and to remove the welded brackets and stiffeners (fairing aids) that were traditionally used to support and align parts of ship structures during assembly. A more recent approach involved cutting out the plates more accurately to ensure a better fit, and then using magnetic or vacuum clamps and hydraulic devices to align them.

Case study 2: Eliminate fettling by improving casting quality

The problem Foundry production of cast pipe components using the 'traditional' green sand casting method resulted in a product (see Figure 6), which required a substantial amount of remedial working, using hand-held grinders, to produce the necessary quality of finish. The holes in the pipe flanges had then to be drilled in a separate operation.

The solution Production of these components was changed to the more modern lost foam casting process.

The result The new process has resulted in such a high quality of casting (see Figure 7) that no fettling is required, thus eliminating all hazardous vibration exposure. In addition, the precision of this casting process allows the holes to be cast into the flanges, eliminating the drilling procedure and further reducing time and cost.

Figure 6   **Figure 7**
Case courtesy of Stanton plc

160 In the maintenance of underground services, electronic detectors have improved the ability to locate leaks from buried pipelines, reducing excessive use of road breakers when exposing fractures for repair. Further increases in productivity and reductions in vibration exposure have been achieved by adopting a 'no dig' strategy for the replacement of ageing, buried pipe systems, instead using techniques for scraping out or splitting the old pipe and relining or replacing the pipe *in situ*.

Reduce exposure by mechanisation

161 Mechanisation and remote control or automation can also help eliminate or reduce exposure. For example, in the foundry industry, productivity has been increased by using manipulators and remote-control swing grinders, allowing more force to be applied during fettling than is possible with a hand-held grinder.

162 Robots are being used increasingly in industry and various organisations have developed robot (or highly-automated) grinders and burning machines for the removal of casting feeder heads and other fettling operations.

Case study 3: Semi-automatic cut-off machine

The problem One of the traditional methods for cutting off cast components is to use an abrasive disc mounted in a circular saw bench. At one foundry an operator could spend up to three hours exposed to vibration levels up to 5 m/s^2. The operation was also noisy and carried a risk of injury from contact with the exposed cutting disc.

The solution Two fully enclosed semi-automatic cut-off machines were bought at a total cost of about £70 000. The multiple castings are clamped in rotating, trunnion-mounted fixtures, and cut off with an abrasive disc. The operator controls the process remotely.

The result

■　Vibration exposure and the risk of injury from the cutting disc are eliminated.

■　Manual handling and exposure to noise, dust and sparks are reduced.

■　The cycle time is cut, improving efficiency.

■　Less fettling is required afterwards, further reducing time and vibration exposure.

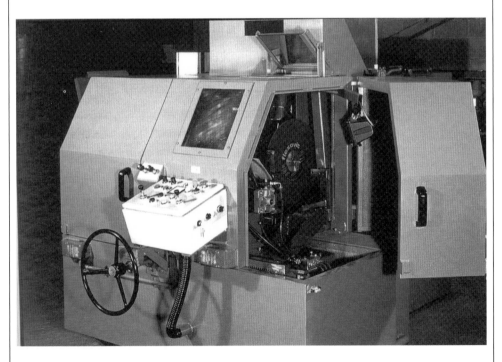

Figure 8
Case courtesy of Flexovit (UK) Ltd

Reduce exposure by good process control

163　Good process control is important for maintaining product quality, production efficiency and controlling vibration exposure. For example, improving the quality control of car-body panel pressing reduces the need for reworking using hand-held orbital and rotary sanders.

Select equipment for reduced vibration exposure

164 After doing all that is reasonably practicable to replace or modify your work processes, your employees may still be exposed to vibration. If so, you should try to avoid unnecessarily high vibration exposures by careful selection of power tools and other equipment. You can do this by:

■ specifying a maximum level of vibration emission as part of your policy when purchasing or renting tools and equipment;

■ asking suppliers, as part of the tendering process, to demonstrate to you and your employees the tools and consumables, such as grinding wheels, in the intended use where the level of vibration can also be measured if required.

165 The efficiency of the tool is important – a tool which takes a long time to do a job will not be popular, and could result in a higher vibration exposure than a more efficient tool with greater vibration emission. Tools may also be too powerful for the job, and this too could result in exposure to unnecessarily high vibration levels.

166 Advances in material and manufacturing technology have brought about improved designs of hand-held and hand-guided machines with lower levels of vibration emission, however, simply buying newer power tools may not eliminate or minimise the vibration exposure. There may still be a residual risk from exposure to vibration which must be managed, and if the tool you choose is not suitable for the job you want to do, it could increase the risk (the Provision and Use of Work Equipment Regulations 1998 apply[12]).

167 Generally, power tools manufactured for professional use can be recognised from their design, appearance and performance. Tools intended for the domestic (DIY) market, where less use is expected, may have greater vibration emissions. All tools on sale in the European Union should meet the relevant safety requirements and carry the 'CE' mark (see 'Information from manufacturers and suppliers of machinery'). You should beware of tools that are copies of well-known brands (so-called grey imports); these may be of a relatively poor standard, unsafe for use and with higher vibration emission.

Power tools – what must I do as an employer?

168 You have duties under the Vibration Regulations to assess the risks to employees from using power tools and to take appropriate measures to control them. The Provision and Use of Work Equipment Regulations 1998 also apply. They require you to provide your employees with equipment which is suitable for the job, to keep it properly maintained and to ensure that operators are trained to use it correctly and safely. The power tool you select must be:

■ suitable for the work it is intended to do and for the conditions in which it will be used;

■ used only for operations and in conditions for which it is suitable;

■ designed and constructed to reduce the risk from vibration;

■ used only by workers trained to use it safely;

■ properly maintained throughout its working life to sustain its best vibration performance.

169 When selecting tools for purchase or hire you should consider ergonomic factors such as:

■ tool weight;

■ tool efficiency and suitability for the task;

■ handle design/comfort;

■ grip force needed;

■ ease of use/handling;

■ cold from grips or exhausts on compressed air tools;

■ noise; and

■ dust.

170 You should take account of your employees' opinions, based on practical trials where possible.

Buying tools - how can manufacturers and suppliers help?

171 Anyone supplying power tools for use in Great Britain (manufacturers, importers, suppliers and tool hire firms) must comply with the Supply of Machinery (Safety) Regulations 1992 (as amended).[6] They have duties to design and construct their products to reduce risks from vibration to a minimum, and to inform you about risks that they have been unable to eliminate by design. They should be able to help you select the most suitable and safe tools for your particular needs by providing useful information and advice about tool vibration, selection and management. See also Part 4 'Information from manufacturers and suppliers of machinery' which should help you to understand the vibration information they supply.

Managing vibration exposure

172 Having selected the most suitable equipment for the work, you should:

■ consider the information/advice you have on risks and how to control them;

■ identify daily limits on actual tool use (ie 'trigger time') so employees can manage their exposures;

■ modify workstations, if necessary, to assure good ergonomics of tool use;

■ discuss and agree with supervisors, safety representatives and operators how the tool is to be used safely, including rules for maximum daily use, and how and when to report any concerns;

■ provide instructions to supervisors and operators;

■ provide training to ensure that operators use the tool in the safest and most efficient way and for no longer than is necessary;

■ restrict use of the equipment to trained operators only;

- set up maintenance and replacement programmes for tools and their consumables (chisels, abrasive discs, drill bits etc); and

- monitor and review these actions regularly.

Maintain tools and equipment

173 Power tools and other work equipment should be serviced and maintained in accordance with the manufacturer's maintenance schedules to prevent unnecessarily high vibration levels and ensure efficient operation. This may include the following:

- keep cutting tools sharp;

- dress grinding wheels correctly;

- replace worn parts;

- carry out necessary balance checks and corrections;

- check and replace defective vibration dampers, bearings and gears;

- sharpen chainsaw teeth and keep the correct chain tension;

- tune and adjust engines.

Reduce the level of vibration transmission to the hand

174 When the use of vibrating equipment and exposure to vibration is unavoidable, it is often possible to control the level of vibration transmitted to the hand. The amount of vibration actually passing into the hand and arm can depend on:

- the level and frequency of vibration of the surfaces which are being held (tools, handles, workpieces etc);

- the position of the hand on the tool, handle or workpiece;

- the forces applied by the hand in gripping, pushing, guiding and supporting the vibrating tool, handle or workpiece;

- ergonomic factors associated with tool use and the operator's posture.

175 Jigs and similar aids incorporating anti-vibration mounts can help avoid the need to grip vibrating surfaces. In some cases the tool manufacturer may supply, or endorse the retrofitting of, 'anti-vibration' handles to their product.

176 Wrapping rubber or other resilient materials around vibrating handles may reduce some vibration at high frequencies, and may improve comfort, but is unlikely to reduce significantly the vibration frequencies which contribute most when the exposure is calculated.

177 The greater the gripping or pushing forces exerted through the hand onto the vibrating surface, the more efficiently the vibration passes into the user's hand and arm. These forces may be necessary to support the tool or workpiece, to control or guide the machine, or to achieve high working rates.

178 The actual forces applied can be greater than is needed for efficient and safe work because of incorrect equipment selection, inadequate maintenance, insufficient operator training or poor workstation design. Some improvements, possibly reducing unnecessarily high gripping and pushing forces, might include the following:

- provide additional support – where heavy workpieces are ground by hand at pedestal grinders, providing a support for the whole piece will mean that the worker needs only to guide it and hold it against the wheel, rather than support all the weight;

- use tension chains (counter-balancers) and manipulators to support vibrating tools such as heavy drills, grinders, nut runners, nailing guns (in some cases) and pneumatic chisels, so that the operator does not have to support the tool's weight;

- change the texture and material of a grip surface so that the operator may be able to use a smaller grip force to hold and control the tool; and

- ensure grinding wheels are 'dressed' to maintain concentricity and balance.

Case study 4: Isolation for pedestal grinding operation

The problem A foundry used a large pedestal grinder to remove flash from aluminium castings. In this operation, the operator holds the casting with both hands and supports it in a fixture while forcing it against the grinding wheel. The fixture was supported by a flimsy fabricated bracket on the body of the grinder. Vibration due to out-of-balance forces in the grinder caused the bracket to resonate and vibration levels of more than 20 m/s^2 were transmitted into the operator's hands through the fixture and casting.

The solution A specialist firm was employed to find a solution. They identified the casting fixture support bracket as the cause of the problem. A more rigid replacement was designed which was mounted directly on the floor and not on the machine. It was made and fitted by the foundry's own staff, at a cost of £20 for materials and half a day's labour.

The result The vibration experienced by the operator was reduced to 1.5 m/s^2, less than a tenth of the original value. In addition, the improved control of the component has resulted in a more consistent finish.

 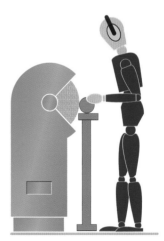

Figure 9 **Figure 10**

Case courtesy of Industrial Noise and Vibration Centre

Reduce the period of exposure

179 When the vibration levels have been reduced so far as is reasonably practicable, further reduction in exposure can only be achieved by limiting the time for which employees are exposed to vibration. This is sometimes necessary to keep exposure below the limit value. It is often helpful to use job rotation (sharing the work and the vibration exposure between several people).

180 Where an employee has a single source of vibration (just one tool or process) it is fairly straightforward to establish a maximum daily exposure duration before, for example, the exposure action or limit value is reached.

181 If an employee uses two or more tools or processes, this is more complex, but the exposure points system, described in Part 2, can be useful to help your supervisors manage your employees' exposures. You can use Table 5, or the exposure 'ready-reckoner' (Table 4), to estimate the number of 'exposure points' per hour for each tool or process. By setting a daily limit on the exposure points for each operator, you can control the daily exposure, even if several different tools or processes contribute to the exposure.

Table 5 Number of exposure points per hour for a range of vibration magnitudes

Vibration (m/s²)	3	4	5	6	7	8	9	10	12	15
Points per hour	18	32	50	72	98	130	160	200	290	450

Note: 100 points/day = exposure action value; 400 points/day = exposure limit value

Example 4: Use of exposure points to control daily exposure

A small engineering firm uses several identical pneumatic angle grinders and, occasionally, a random orbital sander. The company has established that the typical vibration level on the grinders, in normal use, is about 4 m/s². The vibration level on the sander is greater, at about 8 m/s². No other significant sources of HAV are normally used by the company's employees.

The company's policy is to keep the vibration exposures of all its employees below the exposure action value (ie below 100 points per day) and to demonstrate that it is doing this. The manager uses the table and establishes that grinder operators will receive about 30 exposure points per hour and that users of the sander will receive about 130 points per hour.

On this basis the company decides that no employee should be required to operate a grinder for more than a total of three hours per day, or the sander for more than 45 minutes per day. They change the work planning system to ensure this policy is implemented.

The supervisors and all tool operators are given training to explain that the grinders and the sander cause vibration exposure at a rate of 5 and 20 points respectively for every ten minutes of 'trigger time', and that they should not allow their daily total to exceed 100 points. This information is also printed on labels attached to the tools. Worksheets and method statements include an estimated exposure (in points) for the job, and job rotation is specified where required to keep individual exposures below 100 points per day. This allows the operators to use both tools in one day while controlling their exposure; they agree their points total with the supervisor at the end of each day and a record is made.

182 Make sure you maintain an effective level of supervision after introducing new working patterns. It is not uncommon for 'old' work practices to reappear, which can defeat the object of the exercise. Devices are now available which cut off the power supply to pneumatic or electric tools after a specified total operating time. These can help you to control your employees' vibration exposure time, but will still need to be managed carefully.

183 It is believed that employees who are paid by piecework or payment-by-results schemes can be at increased risk. Not only is the period of exposure likely to be intensive and with fewer breaks, but also the rapid pace of work can result in employees applying higher levels of force to the task, increasing the risk of vibration-related ill health and musculoskeletal problems.

Gloves and warm clothing

184 Gloves marketed as 'anti-vibration', which aim to isolate the wearer's hands from the effects of vibration, are available commercially. There are several different types, but many are only suitable for certain tasks, they are not particularly effective at reducing the frequency-weighted vibration associated with risk of HAVS and they can increase the vibration at some frequencies. It is not usually possible to assess the vibration reduction provided in use by anti-vibration gloves, so you should not generally rely on them to provide protection from vibration (more information is in Part 6). However, gloves and other warm clothing can be useful to protect vibration-exposed workers from cold, helping to maintain circulation.

185 Low hand or body temperature increases the risk of finger blanching because of the reduced blood circulation. You should therefore make sure employees working outdoors in cold weather have adequate protection. The temperature in an indoor workplace should provide reasonable comfort without the need for special clothing and should normally be at least 16°C. If this is not reasonably practicable, you should provide warm clothing and gloves.[13] (More than one set may be required for each employee if the gloves or clothing are likely to become wet.) Gloves and other clothing should be assessed for good fit and for effectiveness in keeping the hands and body warm and dry in the working environment. You should also ensure that gloves or other clothing you provide do not stop employees working safely and do not present a risk of entanglement with moving parts of machinery.

Other measures

186 As well as the actions you can take to reduce workers' exposures to vibration, there are other measures which, while not reducing the daily vibration exposure, are thought to reduce the risk. For example:

■ plan employees' work to avoid prolonged exposure and encourage them to take breaks during long tasks, as several shorter exposures with 'recovery' periods are believed to be preferable to one long exposure;

■ keep indoor workplaces as warm and dry as possible;

- provide screening or shelter for outdoor workers in cold, wet or windy conditions;

- provide hot drinks and warm food. This helps to maintain body temperature and is particularly important in cold working environments;

- encourage employees to take regular exercise to help good circulation and to exercise and massage the fingers during breaks from work with vibrating equipment;

- encourage employees to stop or cut down smoking, which can lead to impairment of circulation.

Information and training for operators and supervisors

187 Unless you have succeeded in preventing vibration exposures entirely by eliminating all processes which involve HAV, you will need the co-operation of your workforce to help make your control measures effective. It is important that you provide your operators and their supervisors with information about the risks from vibration and that they receive the required instruction and training in the correct use and maintenance of the equipment (your employees have a duty to co-operate when you take action to comply with health and safety legislation). You should consult employees' safety representatives about the planning and organisation of your health and safety training. See paragraph 78 for more information.

188 They may also need to be trained in working techniques, for example to help avoid excessive gripping, pushing and guiding forces and to ensure the tools are operated safely and with optimum efficiency. With some tools, the operator's hands must be in the correct position to avoid unnecessarily high vibration exposure. Many modern vibration-reduced tools, such as breakers with suspended handles, do not deliver the lower vibration emissions unless they are operated correctly. The manufacturer or supplier should advise you of any training requirements, and may offer training for operators. Workers should also be encouraged to:

- use the lightest tool capable of doing the work safely and efficiently;

- support the tool as much as possible on the material being worked, letting its weight provide the downward force;

- rest hand-held workpieces on any support provided; and

- hold the tool, machine or workpiece with a light but safe grip.

189 Finally, adequate training and supervision will be required to ensure that your workers are adopting the practices listed above for protecting themselves against the development of vibration-related disease. They should be encouraged to report any symptoms (such as numbness, tingling or whiteness of the fingers), which may be associated with exposure to vibration.

190 If your employees are in a health surveillance scheme (see see paragraphs 224-249) you should explain the importance of this, and give them information on the findings. This may provide a regular opportunity for one-to-one discussions of the vibration hazard and how to reduce the risk.

Case study 5: Operator training provided by a breaker manufacturer

A manufacturer of vibration-reduced pneumatic paving breakers made vibration measurements in real working conditions and found that the vibration exposures were highly dependent on the way the machines were operated. The company produced training material for its customers, which included the following points:

- select the correct cutting tool for the job (eg moil point/narrow chisel for concrete; straight-bladed cutter for asphalt) and keep them sharp;

- keep the handles in the horizontal position for lowest vibration (see Figures 11 and 12);

- let the weight of the tool do the work and don't grip too tightly;

- move the cutting tool every 8-10 seconds (the amount of concrete broken is about the same after 10 seconds as after one minute);

- stop the breaker when lifting it to change position because the vibration is high when pulling up on the handles;

- when cutting concrete, take small 'bites' to prevent the cutting tool jamming;

- remove concrete in shallow layers.

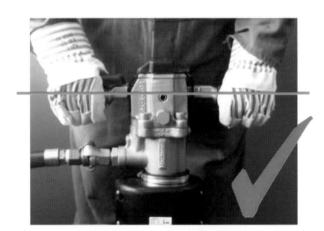

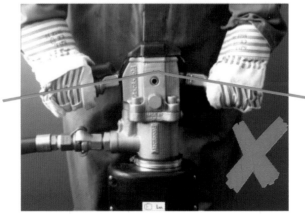

Figures 11 and 12

It was found that, when breaking concrete, untrained operators were lifting the breaker without switching off (so increasing the vibration), and were operating continuously for about a minute without moving the cutting tool. The average vibration was about 9 m/s², which meant that the exposure action value was reached after about 35 minutes trigger time (35 penetrations of the concrete) and the exposure limit value was reached after about 135 minutes trigger time.

By training the operators to stop the machine before moving it, the average vibration was reduced to around 7 m/s², allowing a 70% increase in the time before the exposure action and limit values were reached. Further training improved the operators' techniques and the average vibration was reduced to approximately 5.5 m/s², allowing about 100 minutes trigger time before reaching the exposure action value.

Also, by training the operator to stop and move the cutting tool after about 10 seconds of operating, instead of working continuously for about a minute, the amount of work done (concrete broken) was greatly increased.

The training produced substantial reductions in the vibration exposures, and enabled the operators to use their tools more efficiently. Up to 17 times more concrete could be broken than before, without increasing the vibration exposures.

Case courtesy of Macdonald Air Tools Ltd

Consultation with workers' representatives

191 Discuss with your employees and/or their representatives any proposed changes in the workplace, which might affect their health and safety. This should encourage the co-operation of the operators and supervisors with the control measures you put in place. These discussions may also be helpful when making decisions on control measures and should help you finalise your action plan. Involve them in trials of alternative work processes for reduced vibration or of potential new tools and equipment. A partnership with the workforce when planning control measures will help to ensure that your action plan is workable, that your employees understand it and that they co-operate with your actions to control the risk to their health.

How to obtain competent advice and assistance

192 As an employer you are responsible for assessing the risks from vibration and developing an action plan. This does not have to be done by one individual. For example, you might decide to employ external assistance to help with your vibration risk assessment and to use members of your own staff (who understand your business) to plan and carry out the necessary actions to control the risks from exposure to vibration.

The level of knowledge and expertise required

193 It is important that you (or people helping you) have the necessary expertise to assess exposures and risks from vibration and are able to decide how best to control them. People helping you with your assessment and producing the action plan do not necessarily need an advanced knowledge of vibration or mechanical engineering. However, they should have enough understanding of the subject to tell you if further specialist assistance is required.

Appointing someone from your workforce

194 The ability to understand and apply the guidance in Parts 1-4 of this book is more important than formal qualifications. Someone in your workforce (possibly you) may decide, after reading the appropriate guidance, that they have the ability to assess vibration in your workplace, make recommendations for control of exposure and risk and compile an action plan. You may, however, decide that training is required, particularly if there is likely to be an ongoing requirement for management of vibration risks. Appendix 5 includes information on training courses on assessment and management of hand-arm vibration.

195 While many people will be able to follow the guidance on measurement in Part 2 without additional training, it is not recommended that you attempt to make measurements of hand-arm vibration without the necessary knowledge and experience or without considering a suitably practical training course.

Appointing a consultant

196 You may decide to employ external assistance to help you assess and manage vibration exposures. If you choose to do this, you will need to ensure that they have the necessary skills, knowledge, expertise and experience. HSE has produced a free leaflet INDG322[14] to help you select a consultant to carry out many of the tasks required by health and safety legislation.

Appointing an occupational health service provider

197 If you need health surveillance you will find guidance on selecting suitably qualified people to provide this service in Part 5 'Health surveillance for HAVS'.

PART 4: INFORMATION FROM MANUFACTURERS AND SUPPLIERS OF MACHINERY

- ■ What are the legal duties in relation to designing, manufacturing and supplying vibrating machinery?

- ■ What information should you expect the manufacturer or supplier to provide?

- ■ What are the limitations of this information?

- ■ What test procedures should manufacturers use to measure vibration emission?

198 This section tells you what information and advice you should expect from manufacturers, importers and suppliers (including hire companies) of power tools and other machinery. It also points out special precautions that may be required when interpreting this information.

The Supply of Machinery (Safety) Regulations 1992 (as amended)

199 The Supply of Machinery (Safety) Regulations 1992 as amended,[6] (the SM(S) Regulations) are the implementation in Great Britain of the European Union's 'Machinery Directive' (Directive 98/37/EC) which exists to support the free movement of goods within the European Economic Area (EEA). It establishes essential health and safety requirements for machinery supplied in the EEA, including specific requirements regarding vibration for portable hand-held, hand-guided and mobile machinery.

200 The SM(S) Regulations include essential requirements for manufacturers, importers and suppliers of vibration-emitting machinery to:

- ■ design and construct such machinery so that risks, including those from vibration emissions, are reduced to the lowest level taking account of technical progress;

- ■ provide information to warn you where there are residual risks, ie risks that could not be adequately reduced by design of the equipment;

- ■ provide, in the information/instructions accompanying hand-held or hand-guided machines, information on vibration emissions which reach or exceed 2.5 m/s^2; where the vibration does not exceed 2.5 m/s^2 this must be mentioned;

- ■ provide, in the information/instructions accompanying mobile machines, information on hand-transmitted vibration emissions which reach or exceed 2.5 m/s^2; where the vibration does not exceed 2.5 m/s^2 this must be mentioned.

201 Note that the value of 2.5 m/s^2 referred to above is the vibration emission for a machine and not the daily vibration exposure of the operator. It should **not** be confused with the exposure action value of 2.5 m/s^2 $A(8)$ in the Vibration Regulations.

Reduction of vibration emissions

202 Machinery manufacturers and suppliers are required to design and construct their products so that risks in general are eliminated, or reduced to a minimum, making it possible for your employees to use machinery with the minimum risk to their health or safety. There is a specific requirement that risks from vibration emissions are reduced to the lowest level taking account of technical progress. New tools must be manufactured taking into account the 'state of the art'.

203 Designers and manufacturers should aim to minimise the vibration likely to be generated under all reasonably foreseeable uses (and misuses) of the machine so that people at work are not exposed at levels likely to result in vibration injuries. This will involve the application of effective vibration-reduction techniques by engineering designers. If the risk to the operator is to be kept to a minimum, vibration control and good ergonomic design need to be considered at all stages of design and development of the tool or machine.

Provision of information

204 The SM(S) Regulations require that information on vibration emissions must be provided in instructions accompanying hand-held and hand-guided machinery. There is a similar requirement for mobile machines. The information should:

■ alert you to the vibration emission of machines, and help you select suitable products and design the work processes for which they will be used; and

■ help you plan your arrangements to protect your employees.

205 The main information which must be supplied is:

■ the weighted root-mean-square (rms) acceleration value (ie vibration emission) to which the arms are subjected where this exceeds 2.5 m/s^2 when determined by the appropriate test code (or the fact that it does not exceed 2.5 m/s^2 where this is the case);

■ any measures needed to keep residual risks from vibration under control when the machine is used. For example:

❏ for a chainsaw, if periodic inspection and replacement of the anti-vibration mounts on the handles is required, this should be mentioned in the maintenance instructions;

❏ if the type of inserted tool or consumable (eg grinding disc, blade chisel or drill bit) affects the vibration emission, this should be mentioned in the instructions;

❏ if the vibration emission of a breaker with vibration-isolating handles is dependent on the force applied by the user, advice on the training of operators should be supplied with the machine.

Manufacturers' declared vibration emission values

206 Manufacturers and suppliers have a duty to report vibration emission data, usually according to harmonised European vibration test codes. In Britain these test codes are published as British Standards (see 'References' and 'Further reading').

207 Good-quality vibration emission data can tell you how much vibration is likely to enter a person's hands when using a particular power tool. This is useful to help you to:

- compare the vibration of different brands and models of the same type of tool;

- identify (and avoid) tools that have particularly high vibration emissions;

- consider any significant differences in the vibration of different tools which are, in other respects, suitable for the particular task;

- make an estimate of daily exposure and an assessment of risk, and decide on the need for controlling exposure;

- compare the likely daily exposures with the exposure action and limit values and decide what actions you need to take, for example, limiting the time employees spend on some tasks in any one day.

208 According to BS EN 12096[15] (the Standard which deals with the declaration of vibration emission) two values should be reported by tool manufacturers:

- a (the measured vibration emission); and

- K (the uncertainty of a).

209 This means that a reproduction of the vibration tests used to determine the emission is likely to produce a magnitude of no more than $a + K$. In some cases K can be more than 40% of a, and is often several m/s^2. The difference between the a values for two tools should not be considered significant if it is smaller than one of the quoted K values. For example, tools A and B in the following example should be considered to have the same vibration emission:

Tool A	a = 7 m/s^2	K = 2.7 m/s^2
Tool B	a = 5 m/s^2	K = 2.1 m/s^2

210 Remember, it may not be essential or desirable to choose the tool with the lowest declared vibration emission, as it must also be safe and suitable for the particular task, but you should aim to avoid tools with significantly above average vibration emission.

Limitations of declared emission values

211 At present, some vibration test codes do not represent the way tools perform at work, and vibration levels in the workplace may be much higher than those obtained in this type of 'laboratory' test. This means that the manufacturer's declared vibration emission value may not be representative of real use of the tool. For example:

- vibration is not measured at the handle/hand position producing the greatest emission (eg needle scaler and chipping hammer test codes);

- vibration is measured only in one direction (most current test codes), although the vibration value used to assess exposure and risk is a higher value derived from measurements in three directions (see Part 6);

- the specified direction of measurement is not always the axis of highest magnitude (eg needle scaler, chipping hammer and grinder test codes);

■ the real or simulated operating task specified in the vibration test code generates vibration magnitudes smaller than those likely to be found in normal use (eg grinder test codes).

212 Vibration emission testing of electric, pneumatic and internal combustion powered tools has, in some cases, developed independently in the past. Comparison of vibration emission values obtained using different test codes for tools with different power sources should be made with caution.

213 These concerns have been recognised by the relevant Standards committees. Many harmonised vibration test codes are currently (2005) under review. The revised versions should result in emission values which provide a more accurate guide to likely vibration emissions during 'intended use'. All new and revised test codes should conform with the general principles given in BS EN ISO 20643:2005.[16]

214 Where no test code exists for a specific type of tool, BS EN ISO 20643:2005 can also be used by manufacturers to determine vibration emission. They should select operating conditions for vibration tests with care, and should report the test procedures they have adopted, including:

■ machine configuration, operating and loading conditions during the test; and

■ the positions and directions in which the vibration was measured.

215 Here too, you should be cautious about comparing the vibration emission values declared for different tools that may not have been tested in the same conditions.

216 The examples in the box illustrate the limitations of manufacturers' declared emission values where the vibration test code does not adequately reflect the vibration produced in real use of the tool.

Examples

Interpretation of manufacturers' declared vibration emission values

Vibration magnitudes on hand-held power tools can vary greatly from user to user and task to task, often by factors of 2:1 or 3:1 between the worst and best circumstances. Figure 13 shows ranges of vibration values measured on three tools performing their intended use in the workplace; these are shown by the vertical lines. The average (mean) of these measured values is shown by the mark to the right of the vertical line. The manufacturer's declared emission value, measured using the harmonised test code, and supplied with the tool, is shown by the mark to the left of the vertical line.

For the impact drill the vibration found in 'intended use' varied between 5 and 17 m/s² (with a mean of just over 10 m/s²). This was represented well by the declared emission value of about 12 m/s². In this situation the declared emission value is suitable for estimating daily exposure.

For the chipping hammer the range in 'intended' use was from 10 to 26 m/s² (mean approximately 16 m/s²). The standard emission test for the tool produced a value at the low end of this range, which nevertheless gives a clear indication that vibration emission magnitudes are high and will require management. However, this value would not be suitable to determine the daily operating time before exceeding the exposure action or limit value.

For the rock drill the range in 'intended' use was 15 to 25 m/s² with a mean of about 18 m/s². The emission test produced a value of about 11 m/s² which is below the range of levels measured during 'intended use' and again could not be used directly to show whether the exposure action or limit value is likely to be exceeded.

Despite the large variations found for each of the tools during 'intended use', and the failure of some of the standard tests to produce declared emission values within the range found during 'intended use', each of these tests produced a sufficiently high vibration emission value to demonstrate that daily exposure is likely to exceed the exposure action value (and perhaps the exposure limit value) and to warn of the likely presence of a vibration risk that will require management. (The similarity of the levels found according to the standard emission tests for these three tools is coincidental.)

The vibration data provided by suppliers can help to identify tools with relatively high or low vibration. Figure 14 shows data for two chipping hammers. Both hammers have a large range in their vibration emission depending on the task, etc but it is clear both from the 'intended use' data and the supplier's emission values that one of the hammers is a generally lower vibration tool than the other. However, although the emission value for hammer C helps to identify it as having the lower vibration, it fails to represent the higher vibration levels that will occur in real use and does not identify this tool's potential to expose the operator above the action or limit value.

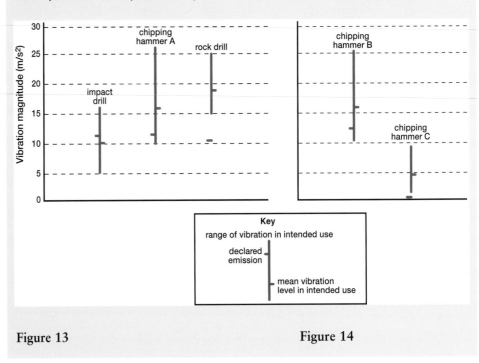

Figure 13   **Figure 14**

217 If the emission value obtained using the appropriate test code is known to be lower than the vibration likely during 'intended use', the supplier should provide further information to warn the user. It is helpful to provide a range of vibration magnitudes likely to be measured in the workplace (vibration total values in accordance with BS EN ISO 5349-1[17]) for a reasonable range of intended uses of the tool, although this is not a specific legal requirement.

Training requirements

218 Some operators of hand-held power tools may require training to ensure that low vibration exposures are achieved and sustained. It may also be necessary to train others such as those who will undertake maintenance of tools. Suppliers have a duty to alert users to particular training that is required. This might include:

■ the need to train operators for new skills for tools with vibration-reduction features (eg correct feed forces for breakers with suspended handles);

■ highlighting any applications of the tool that produce unusually high vibration emissions;

■ information about particular methods of using the tool that greatly affect the emitted vibration; and

■ the need to train maintenance staff to ensure equipment is maintained correctly to prevent vibration from increasing unnecessarily.

Presentation of information, labelling and marking

219 The information on residual risks from vibration (or any other hazards) should be provided in a way that will be understood easily by the user, for example, using labels with readily understandable pictograms or written information in an appropriate language. Warning information should be included in the instructions accompanying the machine and may also appear in catalogues or in separate data sheets. A suggested format for this information is given in Appendix 7.

220 All machinery supplied in accordance with the SM(S) Regulations must be labelled/marked with the following minimum information:

■ the name and address of the manufacturer;

■ CE marking, which includes the year of construction;

■ a description of the machine, including its make, type and serial number; and

■ an indication of the relevant provisions with which the machinery complies.

221 The CE mark indicates that the machinery is designed and manufactured to meet all the relevant essential health and safety requirements in the SM(S) Regulations (the Machinery Directive). These include the duties to minimise risks by design and to provide information on vibration emission and the management of residual risks. The CE mark also indicates that the machine complies with any other Directives that apply to the machine. A Declaration of Conformity must accompany the machine; this will tell you which Directives apply and which Standards were followed in its design and manufacture.

Case study 6: Information provided by a hammer drill and breaker manufacturer

A manufacturer of electric power tools produced vibration emission data for their range of hammer drills and breakers, measured according to the test code BS EN 60745-2-6.

They provided their customers with training material for employees. This covered:

■ selecting the best processes or tools for the job (including, where appropriate, alternatives to drilling or breaking);

■ awareness of risks from vibration;

■ correct operation of reduced-vibration tools, for safety and efficiency;

■ the importance of maintenance and replacement of worn out bits; and

■ information for controlling daily exposure.

Instead of simply stating maximum recommended daily exposure times, the company decided to produce the information in a more useful form, in terms of the work done. Figure 16 the 'drilling selection chart' shows, for each tool type, the recommended drill bit sizes or chisel sizes and the amount of work that can be done in a day before the exposure action value is exceeded. This is expressed (for drills) as the number of holes of 100 mm depth that can be drilled in concrete or (for breakers) the volume of concrete that can be removed.

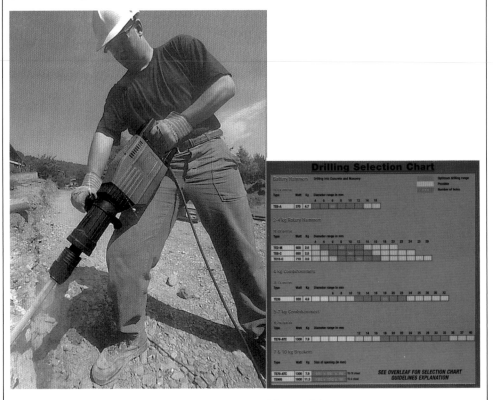

Figure 15   **Figure 16**

Case courtesy of Hilti (Gt. Britain) Ltd

Second-hand equipment

222 The SM(S) Regulations do not apply to machinery first supplied or put into service in the EEA before 1993. However, Section 6 of the Health and Safety at Work etc. Act 1974 requires designers, manufacturers, importers and suppliers of equipment for use at work (including machinery) to ensure, so far as is reasonably practicable, that it is designed and constructed to be safe and without risks to health at all times when it is being set, used, cleaned or maintained by a person at work. They must also provide adequate information on the use for which the equipment is designed so that it can be used safely and without risk to health. Also, under regulation 10 of the Provision and Use of Work Equipment Regulations 1998, machinery you provide for use at work by your employees must comply with the essential health and safety requirements in the SM(S) Regulations.

223 Suppliers of second-hand machinery may be able to rely on information originally supplied with the machine if this is available and sufficient. However, they may need to provide new information if, for example, the original information is no longer available, if the machine has been significantly modified, so that the existing information is no longer valid, or if the original information did not meet the standard required.

PART 5: HEALTH SURVEILLANCE FOR HAVS

- ■ What are the health effects?

- ■ What do I have to do as an employer?

- ■ How do I find qualified people to help me?

What is health surveillance?

224 Health surveillance is about having procedures to detect work-related ill health at an early stage and acting on the results. The main aims are to safeguard the health of employees (including identifying and protecting people at increased risk), and also to check the long-term effectiveness of control measures. In the case of hand-arm vibration, one of the specific aims is to prevent employees developing an advanced stage of hand-arm vibration syndrome (HAVS) associated with disabling loss of hand function. It is possible that your employees who are exposed to vibration may have mild symptoms of HAVS. If they are not aware that they have the disease, health surveillance can help them to recognise that the first symptoms of HAVS have started to develop.

What are the health effects?

225 Employees whose hands are regularly exposed to vibration may suffer from damage to the tissues of hands and arms, which causes the symptoms collectively known as HAVS. These symptoms include:

- ■ numbness and tingling in the fingers, and a reduced sense of touch and temperature, due to damage to nerves in the hand. This damage can make it difficult to feel, and to work with, small objects;

- ■ periodic attacks during which the blood circulation in the fingers is impaired and parts of the fingers become white (blanched). This is sometimes known as 'vibration white finger', 'dead finger' or 'dead hand'. During these attacks the fingers feel numb. As blood circulation returns to normal, either by itself or after rewarming the fingers, they are typically throbbing, red and painful. Although vibration causes the condition, it does not bring on the attacks. The main trigger for these symptoms is exposure to the cold, eg being outdoors early on a winter's morning, or by localised or general body cooling in otherwise warm environments. Rarely, in very advanced cases, blood circulation may be permanently affected;

- ■ joint pain and stiffness in the hand and arm. Grip strength can be reduced due to nerve and muscle damage.

226 An individual employee with HAVS may not experience the complete range of symptoms, eg there may be nerve damage symptoms without there being blood circulation problems and vice versa. The symptoms of HAVS are usually progressive as exposure to vibration continues, eg the effects on blood circulation are seen initially in the tips of the affected fingers, with changes spreading up the finger. The thumb may also be affected.

227 Carpal tunnel syndrome, a disorder of the hand and arm which may involve tingling, numbness, pain and weakness in parts of the hand, can also be caused by exposure to vibration.

228 Employees suffering from HAVS can experience difficulty in carrying out tasks in the workplace involving fine work or manipulative work and are less able to work in cold conditions. The disease may have an impact on earnings and on social and family life. Everyday tasks may become difficult, eg fastening small buttons on clothes. Attacks of 'white finger' will take place not only at work, but during other activities, especially if people get cold, such as when washing the car or watching outdoor sports. The damage to the hands may be irreversible.

229 After symptoms first appear, generally the longer an employee is exposed to vibration, the worse the symptoms become, although the rate of deterioration will vary from person to person. How much symptoms may improve when people are no longer exposed to vibration is not well understood, but it is thought that nerve damage does not improve after exposure stops. The effects on blood circulation may improve after reducing or stopping vibration exposure in people below about 45 years old and when the disease has not yet reached the advanced stage associated with disability. Any improvement will be slow, taking several years and smoking may also slow down recovery.

When is health surveillance required?

230 Health surveillance should be provided for vibration-exposed employees who:

- are likely to be regularly exposed above the action value of 2.5 m/s^2 $A(8)$;

- are likely to be exposed occasionally above the action value and where the risk assessment identifies that the frequency and severity of exposure may pose a risk to health; or

- have a diagnosis of HAVS (even when exposed below the action value).

231 If you are self-employed there is no legal requirement for you to have health surveillance for HAVS. However, it is important for your well-being, and for your ability to remain in work, that you identify any early signs of HAVS and take appropriate action. It is therefore recommended that you follow this guidance if you think you are at risk from vibration.

What do I actually have to do?

232 You need to ensure that you achieve an effective health surveillance programme in the workplace, including co-operation from employees.

233 When you plan to introduce health surveillance, explain to your employees and their safety or employee representatives what you are proposing to do and give them the opportunity to comment on your proposals. Employees need to be given information about the reasons for carrying out health surveillance and they need to understand their roles and responsibilities.

A simple approach to health surveillance

234 A simple approach to health surveillance involves working through a number of stages. Briefly, this 'tiered' system works as follows:

Tier 1 is a short questionnaire (see Appendix 2) used as a first check for people moving into jobs involving exposure to vibration. The replies to the questionnaire will indicate whether they need to be referred to Tier 3 for a HAVS health assessment.

Tier 2 is a short questionnaire (see Appendix 3) that you can issue once a year to employees exposed to vibration risks to check whether they need to be referred to Tier 3 for a HAVS health assessment.

Tier 3 involves a HAVS health assessment by a qualified person (eg an occupational health nurse). If the assessment shows that the employee has HAVS, Tier 4 will apply.

Tier 4 involves a formal diagnosis and is carried out by a doctor qualified in occupational health. The doctor will advise you on the employee's fitness for work.

Tier 5 is optional and involves referral of the employee for certain tests for HAVS. The results may help the doctor assess fitness for work.

235 It may help you keep costs down if you adopt this approach. If you have any positive responses at Tier 1 or 2 which means moving on to Tier 3, you will need to use qualified occupational health professionals but it is not necessary for each employee to be referred to them. In this tiered approach, most appointments with specialists are limited to cases where symptoms that may be suggestive of HAVS have been reported.

'Responsible person'

236 It is useful to appoint a 'responsible person' as part of your health surveillance programme (Tier 2) to help explain to the employees how the simple screening questionnaire operates. This person:

- should be carefully selected to have experience of the working environment and be able to gain the confidence and co-operation of employees;

- need not be qualified but should have received training from an occupational health professional;

- should understand the health surveillance procedures and the importance of confidentiality;

- should be able to describe to the employee the symptoms of HAVS but should not attempt to diagnose disease;

- should not make judgements about the cause of the symptoms if an employee discloses that they have symptoms.

What do I do with completed questionnaires?

237 Completed questionnaires could be sorted, and referrals handled in house, by the responsible person, as long as this is acceptable to employees. However, it may be appropriate for the questionnaires to be treated as confidential and returned to suitably competent health professionals. In the first instance, any employee reporting symptoms should be referred to a 'qualified person' (usually an occupational health nurse) for clinical assessment (Tier 3). The qualified person can make an informed assessment of the nature of reported symptoms on the basis of a confidential interview and limited medical examination. A formal diagnosis of HAVS should only be made by a competent doctor (Tier 4). An employee with HAVS should be reassessed at regular intervals and may need additional investigations in order to detect any progression of the disease.

How do I find someone who is suitably qualified?

238 You should make sure that nurses and doctors offering to carry out health surveillance have appropriate qualifications and training and will provide you with appropriate information. If there is a lack of competence, mistakes have the potential for serious consequences for you and your employees.

239 Appropriate occupational health qualifications for health surveillance of HAVS are:

■ for doctors: Diploma, Associateship or Membership of the Faculty of Occupational Medicine (DipOm, AFOM, MFOM);

■ for nurses: Diploma or Degree in Occupational Health or MSc; **plus**

■ certification for both doctors and nurses from a Faculty of Occupational Medicine approved training course in HAV (see Appendix 6) or equivalent level of competency.

240 For further advice see HSE's guidance book *Health surveillance at work* (HSG61)[18] which describes the roles of the responsible person, qualified person and doctor.

241 For a limited period, following the introduction of the Vibration Regulations in 2005, you may need to use health professionals who have not yet had the specialist training approved by the Faculty. They should, however, possess general occupational health or medicine qualifications and be familiar with the guidance for health professionals in Part 7.

What information will I receive?

242 An employee found to have HAVS should be informed of this by an appropriate health professional. You can be told about an individual employee being diagnosed with HAVS, as long as the employee gives their consent. You may receive advice about any recommended restrictions that relate to the employee's job. Even if the individual does not give consent for medical information to be passed on, you should receive advice on fitness for work with exposure to vibration for each employee undergoing health surveillance. You should also expect to obtain anonymised information, eg for groups of employees.

What do I need to do about the results of health surveillance?

243 You need to make a decision about an individual employee if the doctor advises you that they are not fit for work with exposure to vibration. The employee is at risk of developing disabling loss of hand function if exposure is allowed to continue. You should consider assigning the employee to alternative work where there is no risk from further exposure to vibration.

244 If you are informed that an employee has been diagnosed with HAVS but is still fit for work with exposure to vibration, it is good practice for you to consider taking further action to reduce that employee's exposure.

245 Health surveillance results should be used to check the long-term effectiveness of your control measures. If the number of employees with HAVS has increased, or if the disease is progressing in affected individuals, you need to review your risk assessment and action plan.

What if no symptoms are reported?

246 If no symptoms are reported on the screening questionnaire, there is no need to refer the employee for further assessment, but they should complete the simple questionnaire again on an annual basis (Tier 2). HSE recommends that after three years of a vibration-exposed employee reporting no symptoms they should be referred for a consultation with an occupational health nurse to provide an opportunity to explore more fully any possible symptoms that the individual may have overlooked.

What type of records should I keep?

247 You should keep a health record for each individual for as long as they are under health surveillance, although you may wish to retain it for longer. It is good practice to offer individual employees a copy of their health records when they leave your employment, if your business should cease trading or the employee ceases to be exposed to vibration. The record should be kept up to date and should include:

- identification details of the employee;

- the employee's history of exposure to vibration;

- the outcome of previous health surveillance in terms of fitness for work, and any restrictions required;

- the Tier 1 and Tier 2 questionnaire results (as long as they are not confidential) even if an employee has said they have no symptoms.

248 Health records should not contain personal medical information which must be kept in confidence in the medical record held by the occupational health professional. The enforcing authority is entitled to ask to see your health records as part of their checks that you are complying with the Vibration Regulations.

Could an occupational health service provider carry out a complete health surveillance service?

249 You could ask an occupational health service provider to provide a complete service on your behalf. They should be able to:

- advise you on a suitable health surveillance programme for your employees;

- set up the programme;

- provide the necessary training and supervision for your staff if they are going to help with the basic health surveillance;

- provide suitably qualified and experienced staff to carry out Tiers 3, 4 and 5 of the health surveillance;

- provide you with reports on your employees' fitness to continue work with vibration exposure.

RIDDOR reporting

250 The Reporting of Injuries, Diseases and Dangerous Occurrences Regulations 1995 (RIDDOR) place a duty on you as an employer to report any cases of HAVS arising from certain work activities or of carpal tunnel syndrome associated with exposure to vibration. The duty comes into effect when you receive a formal written diagnosis from a doctor confirming that the employee has either of these conditions and that there is reason to believe that the disease is likely to have an occupational origin. Before reporting HAVS to the Incident Contact Centre (Tel: 0845 300 9923 or website www.riddor.gov.uk), you should check that the employee is currently doing a job involving one of the specific activities listed in Schedule 3 of RIDDOR (see Appendix 1). You are also required to keep details of any report you make for at least three years.

Industrial Injuries Disablement Benefit (IIDB) Scheme

251 It may also be appropriate for you to advise your employee that the vascular form of vibration white finger and carpal tunnel syndrome are both prescribed diseases under the Industrial Injuries Disablement Benefit (IIDB) Scheme. More information is available from Jobcentreplus.

PART 6: TECHNICAL GUIDANCE FOR HEALTH AND SAFETY ADVISORS AND SPECIALISTS

252 The guidance for employers in Parts 2, 3 and 4 will often be enough to help them assess the risk from vibration exposure with sufficient accuracy and precision and to determine what they need to do to comply with the Vibration Regulations. Part 6 contains additional guidance for those providing employers with advice or technical services. It supplements the guidance for employers in Part 2, 3 and 4.

Evaluation of daily vibration exposure

253 Exposure to hand-arm vibration should be evaluated in accordance with BS EN ISO 5349-1:2001.[17] Additional, more detailed, guidance on vibration exposure evaluation (including practical information on the measurement of vibration) is given in BS EN ISO 5349-2:2002.[19]

254 A person's daily vibration exposure depends on the vibration magnitudes to which they are exposed and on how long the exposures last. The Vibration Regulations (Schedule 1) use the definition of daily vibration exposure given in BS EN ISO 5349-1:2001. Daily exposures are expressed as 'eight-hour energy-equivalent' vibration magnitudes ($A(8)$ values). Exposures expressed in this way can be compared with one another and with the exposure action value and the exposure limit value in the Vibration Regulations. The $A(8)$ value is the vibration magnitude (frequency-weighted root-mean-square (rms) acceleration in m/s^2) which, if maintained constant for a period of eight hours, would be equivalent, in energy terms, to the actual vibration for the actual exposure time.

Vibration magnitude

255 The vibration magnitude produced in many work processes is variable. It can depend on the design, configuration and condition of the vibrating tool or equipment, the workpiece or material being worked, and the physical characteristics and technique of the operator, and can also change significantly over time. It is therefore necessary to find a value (or range of values) to represent the average magnitude of vibration to which the hand is exposed during the work process. This value is the three axis vibration total value, a_{hv}, as defined in BS EN ISO 5349-1:2001 (see Figure 19 in the 'Vibration measurement and instrumentation' section).

256 There are many sources of information on likely vibration magnitudes which can be used to estimate exposures. These include advice provided by manufacturers of power tools and other machinery trade associations and others who have experience with the work processes and tools used. However, sometimes there may be no suitable information available on the vibration magnitudes likely in the work you are assessing. It will then be necessary to make measurements in the workplace.

Daily exposure duration

257 Before the exposure can be calculated, the total daily duration of exposure to the vibration from a tool or process must be obtained. It is important to remember that this is the actual time for which the hands are actually exposed to the measured magnitude of vibration from the tool, machine or workpiece. This is sometimes called the contact time or trigger time and is often over-estimated by tool operators.

258 For processes where the tool or process is operated for long periods in the day, the daily exposure duration can be estimated by observing the work during a representative part of the working day and noting how much of the time the tool is operating. A stopwatch or video recording can be useful for this.

259 If the vibration is intermittent, the total exposure duration can be more difficult to estimate. However, for regular repetitive operations (such as in the manufacturing or processing of identical components) you will usually have access to information on the number of such operations occurring in a day. If an average duration for an operation is established by observation, the total daily duration can then be estimated.

Matching the magnitude to the duration

260 In some operations, the vibration occurs in short bursts (eg work with riveting hammers or impact wrenches) and the sampling strategy during a vibration measurement will affect the measured magnitude. If, for example, rms vibration values are obtained from measurements made over periods of 60 seconds, during which five short riveting operations take place, then you can use a notional exposure duration of twelve seconds per rivet (ie 60 divided by 5 is 12) when determining a daily exposure from that measured vibration magnitude. If the measurements are made only during the shorter periods when the tool is operating, the measured magnitude will be greater but the corresponding exposure duration is the true 'trigger time'; this is usually more difficult to assess accurately. Caution is therefore required when using vibration magnitude data measured by someone else.

Uncertainty

261 Whether you have obtained your average vibration magnitude through measurement in the workplace or from other information, this value, and the daily exposure you derive from it, will be subject to uncertainty. Research conducted for HSE has shown that errors arising from the process of sampling and measuring vibration magnitude, and estimating exposure duration, can result in an uncertainty in the $A(8)$ value of at least ±20%. To comply with the Vibration Regulations you do not need to produce exposure values with high precision, but if your estimated exposures are close to the exposure action or limit value, then you should assume that it is **likely** that they will be exceeded and the employer should take the appropriate action to reduce the exposure and control the risk and start health surveillance.

Calculating the vibration exposure

262 The vibration exposure for the daily use of a process or tool is calculated from a magnitude and a duration, using this equation:

Equation 1

$$A(8) = a_{hv} \sqrt{\frac{T}{T_0}}$$

where a_{hv} is the vibration magnitude (in m/s^2), T is the daily duration of exposure to the vibration magnitude a_{hv} and T_0 is the reference duration of eight hours. (Note that, because of the square root term, changes and uncertainties in exposure duration have a smaller effect on the $A(8)$ value than similar changes and uncertainties in vibration magnitude.)

Partial vibration exposures

263 If a worker is exposed to vibration from more than one source of vibration (perhaps because they use two or more different tools or processes during the day) then a partial vibration exposure is obtained from the magnitude and duration for each one. These values are then combined to give the overall daily exposure value, $A(8)$, for that person:

Equation 2

$$A(8) = \sqrt{A_1(8)^2 + A_2(8)^2 + A_3(8)^2 + \ldots}$$

where $A_1(8)$, $A_2(8)$, $A_3(8)$ etc are the partial vibration exposure values for the different vibration sources, each calculated using Equation 1.

264 Partial exposure values will help you advise the employer to set priorities when developing the action plan – a partial exposure which dominates the overall value of $A(8)$ should be given priority.

The exposure points system

265 Some employers find it useful to monitor and control their employees' vibration exposures by recording and limiting the time they spend using tools or doing jobs involving vibration exposure. However, because the exposure time is not directly proportional to the daily vibration exposure (or $A(8)$ value) this can be complicated to manage, especially when a person is exposed to vibration from two or more sources in one day.

266 Assessment and subsequent management of exposures can be simplified by using the exposure points system. Unlike the process of adding $A(8)$ values (see Equation 2), exposure points can be added using simple arithmetic. The number of exposure points per hour of use (or any convenient period of time) can be established for a type of power tool or work process, from its vibration magnitude. This provides employers with a simple method of recording and controlling vibration exposures. HSE's suggested exposure points system is also described in paragraphs 133-134.

267 The number of exposure points, n, is defined by:

Equation 3

$$n = \left[\frac{a_{hv}}{2.5} \right]^2 \times \frac{t}{8} \times 100$$

where a_{hv} is the vibration magnitude in m/s^2 and t is the exposure time in hours.

268 The $A(8)$ value is related to the number of points as follows:

Equation 4

$$A(8) = 2.5 \times \sqrt{\frac{n}{100}}$$

269 The exposure scores corresponding to the exposure action and limit values are then:

■   exposure action value (2.5 m/s² $A(8)$) = 100 points;

■   exposure limit value (5 m/s² $A(8)$) = 400 points.

270 For any particular tool or process, the number of exposure points accumulated in an hour (n_{1h}) can be obtained from the vibration magnitude using Equation 3:

Equation 5

$$n_{1h} = 2\, a_{hv}{}^2$$

Tools for calculating daily exposure

Ready-reckoner

271 In practice, most employers and their advisors will not wish to take the mathematical route (using equations) to calculating exposures. Part 2 contains a 'ready-reckoner' for daily exposures. This allows a partial exposure to be obtained if the vibration magnitude and exposure duration are known. These values are exposure points, which can be added to obtain an individual's overall daily exposure.

272 To avoid giving the user an inappropriate impression of precision when calculating daily exposures, the values in the ready-reckoner table have been rounded to $2^1/_2$ significant figures (or the nearest integer for values of less than 100).

273 The cells in the table are colour-coded with red for exposures above the exposure limit value, green for exposures below the exposure action value and yellow for exposures between the two. Two further colours have been included: light green representing exposures above 2 m/s² $A(8)$ (64 points), and orange representing exposure above 4 m/s² $A(8)$ (255 points). Because of the uncertainties associated with daily exposure values (at least ±20%) it should be considered **likely**, for values in these ranges, that the daily exposure will exceed the exposure action value or exposure limit value respectively.

The on-line calculator

274 An exposure calculator (Microsoft Excel spreadsheet) is available on HSE's vibration page pages at www.hse.gov.uk/vibration (see Part 2). It uses the above equations to calculate partial exposures for up to six pairs of magnitude and duration values together with the total daily exposure. All exposures are displayed as $A(8)$ values (rounded to one decimal place) and as exposure points (rounded to the nearest integer value).

275 The calculator also uses the vibration magnitudes entered by the user to calculate (to the nearest minute) the time required to reach the exposure action and limit values using, respectively:

Equation 6

$$t_{EAV} = \frac{2.5^2 \times 8}{a_{hv}^2}$$

and

Equation 7

$$t_{ELV} = \frac{5^2 \times 8}{a_{hv}^2}$$

where t_{EAV} and t_{ELV} are in hours.

The nomogram

276 The nomogram in Figure 17 provides another simple method for obtaining exposures, without using the equations.

277 For each work activity (tool, machine or process) draw a line from a point on the left-hand scale (representing the vibration magnitude in m/s²) to a point on the right-hand scale (representing the exposure duration). Read off the partial exposure, as an $A(8)$ value or number of exposure points, where the lines cross the central scale. To combine all the partial exposures, and get the overall daily exposure value, square the partial $A(8)$ values, add them and take the square root of the result (see Equation 2); alternatively, simply add the exposure points for each partial exposure.

Weekly average of daily vibration exposure

278 In certain circumstances (when the daily exposure is usually below the exposure action value, but varies markedly and may occasionally exceed the exposure limit value) the Vibration Regulations allow the exposure to be averaged over a week for the purposes of comparison with the exposure limit value. The weekly average vibration exposure is defined in Schedule 1 to the Regulations by:

Equation 8

$$A(8)_{week} = \sqrt{\frac{1}{5} \sum_{j=1}^{7} A(8)_j^2}$$

where $A(8)_j$ is the daily exposure for day j. To calculate the weekly average, $A(8)_{week}$:

1 Square each of the daily exposures $A(8)_j$ for seven consecutive days.

2 Add the squared values together.

3 Divide by 5.

4 Take the square root of the result.

279 The value obtained for $A(8)_{week}$ may be compared with the exposure limit value in the usual way.

280 You should note that the use of weekly exposures is rarely appropriate except in exceptional or unexpected situations – such as occasional operations by the emergency services. When the daily vibration exposure is very different from day to day, it will often be reasonably practicable to plan the work to spread the exposure across more days.

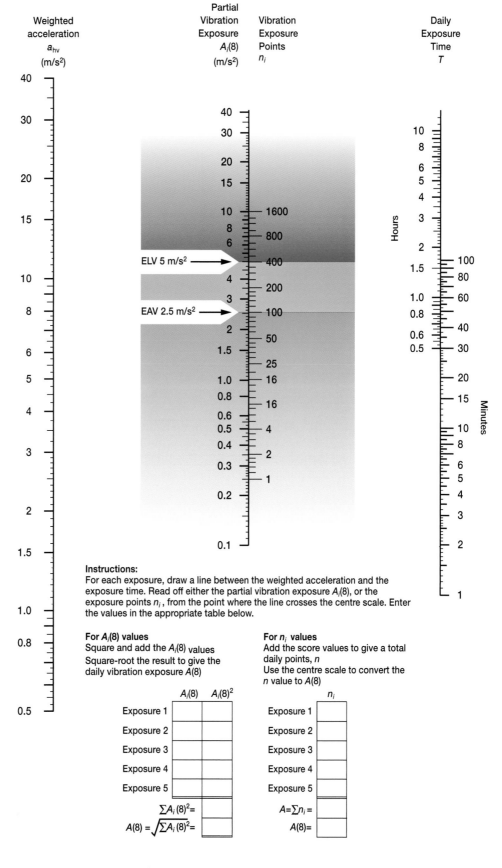

Figure 17 Nomogram for calculating daily vibration exposure

Vibration measurement and instrumentation

281 Anyone making hand-arm vibration measurements should be familiar with BS EN ISO 5349-1:2001 and BS EN ISO 5349-2:2002 which contain detailed practical guidance on measurement of vibration in the workplace.

What is measured?

282 The vibration magnitude (level) is represented by the frequency-weighted rms acceleration in m/s² of the surface of the tool, handle or workpiece in contact with the hand.

Frequency weighting

283 The risk to health from vibration is affected by the frequency content of the vibration. When vibration is measured in accordance with BS EN ISO 5349-1:2001, vibration frequencies between 8 and 16 Hz are given most weight, and frequencies above and below this range make a smaller contribution to the measured vibration magnitude. This process is called frequency weighting. Vibration meters intended for HAV measurement are equipped with a frequency weighting filter, to modify their sensitivity at different frequencies of vibration.

Averaging

284 During a vibration measurement, the rms value of the frequency-weighted acceleration is determined. It is important that the measurement duration is long enough to allow a representative average value to be obtained.

285 Measurements should be made to produce vibration values that represent the average vibration for that tool or process throughout the operator's working period during the day. It is therefore important that the operating conditions and measurement periods etc. are selected to achieve this.

Measurement positions and directions

286 At each hand position on the tool, handle, workpiece etc the vibration is measured in three separate directions (known as the x-, y- and z-axes) at right-angles to one another (see Figure 18). It is preferable to measure in all three directions at the same time.

287 For exposure evaluation, the three frequency-weighted rms acceleration values (a_{hwx}, a_{hwy} and a_{hwz}) are combined to give an overall frequency-weighted vibration magnitude, a_{hv}, using:

Equation 9

$$a_{hv} = \sqrt{a_{hwx}^2 + a_{hwy}^2 + a_{hwz}^2}$$

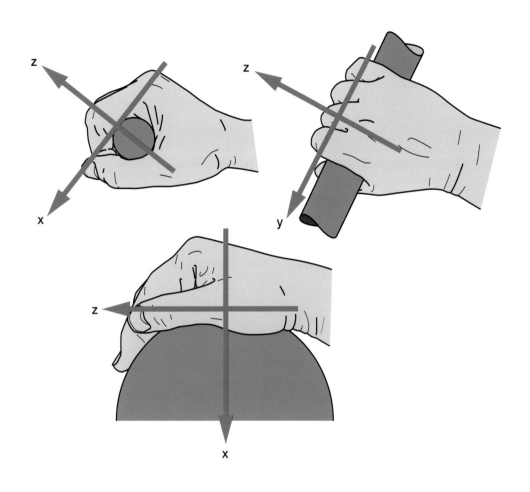

Figure 18 Directions of vibration measurement

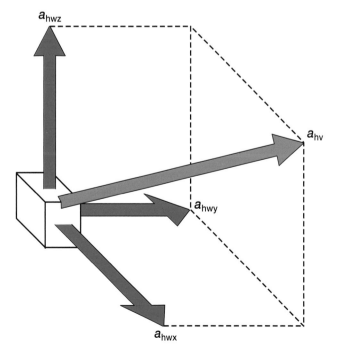

Figure 19 The vibration total value a_{hv}

288 This is the three-axis vibration total value, sometimes referred to as the 'root-sum-of-squares' or the 'vector sum' (see Figure 19). This value (at the hand position with the greatest vibration) is used to calculate the daily vibration exposure ($A(8)$ value) of the worker* for comparison with the exposure action and limit values.

Instruments for vibration measurement

289 Vibration meters and other items of measuring equipment should meet the correct specification for the measurement of hand-transmitted vibration given in BS EN ISO 8041:2005.[20] Accelerometers (vibration transducers) and the accessories and methods for mounting them should be carefully selected; BS EN ISO 5349-2:2002 contains useful guidance. Suppliers of vibration-measuring instruments should be able to advise on the selection of equipment suitable for the purpose.

Technical guidance on anti-vibration gloves

290 Several different types of anti-vibration gloves are available, although many are only suitable for a restricted range of activities and they are not generally effective at reducing the frequency-weighted vibration (ie vibration at the frequencies that have the greatest effect on vibration exposure).

291 The degree of vibration reduction provided by gloves depends on the thickness and softness of the lining, which is usually a resilient gel, foam or rubber-like material or an array of air bladders. To protect against lower vibration frequencies the contact areas of the glove need to contain thicker resilient material. This may seriously limit dexterity and comfort and the gloves may therefore be unsafe to use and unacceptable to employees. Gloves may also result in operators having to tighten their grip on the tool and, as a result, actually increase the risk of vibration injury.

292 Gloves marketed in Europe as 'anti-vibration' must carry the CE mark, indicating they have been tested and found to meet the requirements of the current standard, BS EN ISO 10819:1997 (under revision in 2005).[21]

293 This standard requires that anti-vibration gloves:

■ **on average**, provide some protection against relatively high vibration frequencies (200 Hz and above); and
■ do not, **on average**, increase vibration levels at lower frequencies.

294 These requirements mean that the specified vibration reductions are not defined for individual vibration frequencies, but are based on the average over a wide range of frequencies. Therefore, some gloves may increase, rather than reduce, vibration at particular frequencies and still meet the requirements of the standard. This could result in an **increase** in the overall vibration exposure if the tool or process happens to vibrate at the glove's resonance frequency.

---

* According to the previous British and International Standards on evaluation of HAV exposure (BS 6842:1987 and ISO 5349:1986, both now withdrawn) vibration was measured in three directions, but the exposure was determined from the greatest of the three values. The former HSE guidance on HAV (HSG88, 1994) gave a daily exposure 'action level' of 2.8 m/s² $A(8)$ which was also based on this 'dominant axis' value. Use of the vibration total value, as required by the Vibration Regulations and the current Standard (BS EN ISO 5349-1:2001), results in slightly greater vibration magnitudes than before.

295 Gloves will generally perform best at the higher frequencies, with little effect at low and medium frequencies. This means they can pass the standard test and still produce only negligible or moderate reductions in the frequency-weighted vibration magnitude at the hand. This is because of the shape of the frequency weighting which assumes that the lower frequencies of vibration have the greatest effect on health.

296 The standard test considers only the reduction of vibration in one direction, at the palm of the hand. There is no information about the performance of the glove in three directions, or at the fingers. In practice this means that it is not usually possible to predict a 'protected' level of vibration exposure inside the glove.

297 The absence of detailed performance data for gloves means it is difficult for employers to assess adequately the protection given by anti-vibration gloves, as required by the Personal Protective Equipment at Work Regulations 1992.[22] Additional testing of the vibration characteristics of the tool or process, in combination with the glove, would be required and experience to date has shown that the results are generally disappointing. (Exceptionally, testing may show that the gloves are likely to be effective in specific circumstances, but this should be demonstrated, and all other reasonably practicable exposure control measures are still required under the Vibration Regulations.)

298 Manufacturers continue to conduct research to develop materials for gloves, which can provide substantial reductions in vibration across a wider range of frequencies. Work is also currently being undertaken to improve BS EN ISO 10819:1997. A revised standard may require glove manufacturers in the future to provide better information with which to compare gloves and assess the protection they provide. However, it remains unlikely that an adequate assessment will be possible using standardised information provided by the supplier.

299 In the meantime, employers should not assume anti-vibration gloves will reduce vibration exposures unless test data confirms this for the particular combination of glove and tool used. Gloves may be a useful supplementary measure which, at least, ensures that operators protect their hands and keep them warm, and may be beneficial in reducing the higher frequencies of vibration. However, anti-vibration gloves alone should not be relied on to significantly reduce vibration exposures. A pair of good quality industrial gloves will often provide equal levels of protection.

300 Before recommending the use of anti-vibration gloves, work through the following checklist:

■ list the tools which still contribute significantly to vibration exposure (after all other reasonably practicable control measures have been taken);

■ estimate how much lower the vibration magnitudes have to be before the exposures are reduced to below the exposure action value;

■ ask the supplier about glove performance in relation to these requirements;

■ examine glove test data (seek help in interpreting it, if necessary);

■ check with the supplier that their gloves are suitable for the tools used;

■ check whether the gloves are acceptable to employees;

- check that employees can maintain the necessary levels of dexterity when wearing the gloves;

- confirm the gloves adequately protect employees from other risks – such as cuts and abrasions or exposure to chemicals;

- check how long they are expected to last in normal use and the cost of regular replacement.

PART 7: GUIDANCE ON HEALTH SURVEILLANCE FOR OCCUPATIONAL HEALTH PROFESSIONALS

301 This section advises health professionals on the clinical effects of hand-arm vibration and the implementation of a health surveillance programme for employees exposed to vibration.

Clinical effects

302 Employees whose hands are regularly exposed to vibration may suffer from symptoms due to pathological effects on the peripheral vascular system, peripheral nervous system, muscles and other tissues of the hand and arm. The symptoms are collectively known as hand-arm vibration syndrome (HAVS).

Neurological component

303 Neurological symptoms of HAVS include numbness and tingling in the fingers, and a reduced sense of touch and temperature. This nerve damage can be disabling, making it difficult to feel, and to work with, small objects.

Vascular component

304 Episodic finger blanching is the characteristic vascular sign. This is sometimes known as 'vibration white finger', 'dead finger' or 'dead hand'. The main trigger for the symptoms is exposure to the cold, for example being outdoors early on a winter's morning. The symptoms can also be triggered by localised or general body cooling in otherwise warm environments. Although vibration causes the condition, it does not precipitate the symptoms.

305 After initial blanching indicating vasospasm, the circulation is restored, either spontaneously (after a variable period of time that can be from several minutes to an hour or more) or after rewarming the fingers. Tissue ischaemia occurs during the period of spasm. This leads to an exaggerated return of blood flow and painful red throbbing fingers (reactive hyperaemia). During attacks the sufferer may complain of numbness, pain and cold as well as reduced manual dexterity. Effects are seen initially in the tips of the affected fingers, with changes then spreading up the finger with continuing exposure. The thumb may also be affected. As the condition progresses, the frequency of attack will increase. Rarely, in very severe cases, blood circulation may be permanently impaired.

Muscular and soft tissue component

306 Employees may complain of joint pain and stiffness in the hand and arm. Grip strength can be reduced due to nerve and muscle damage.

307 An individual employee suffering from HAVS may not experience the complete range of symptoms, for example symptoms related to the neurological component can be present in the absence of vascular problems and vice versa. Neurological symptoms generally appear earlier than finger blanching.

308 Carpal tunnel syndrome, a disorder of the hand and arm giving rise to tingling, numbness, weakness, pain and night waking, can be caused by exposure to vibration.

309 Employees suffering from HAVS can experience difficulty in carrying out tasks in the workplace involving fine work or manipulative work and have a

reduced ability to work in cold conditions. The disease may also have an impact on social and family life. Periodic attacks of 'white finger' will take place not only at work, but also during activities such as car washing or watching outdoor sports. Everyday tasks, for example fastening small buttons on clothes, may become difficult.

Prognosis

310 The symptoms of HAVS are usually progressive with continuing exposure to vibration. There will be individual variation in the timing and rate of deterioration. The degree to which symptoms regress on removal from exposure to vibration is not known with any certainty and the condition may be irreversible. There is limited evidence to indicate that neurological symptoms do not improve. Vascular symptoms may show improvement after reducing or ceasing vibration exposure in patients below about 45 years of age and when the disease has not yet reached the advanced stage associated with disability. Any improvement is, however, slow, taking several years. Smoking may undermine recovery in these individuals. The vascular symptoms do not normally get worse after discontinuing exposure to vibration and in people where deterioration does arise this may be associated with other conditions (for example, collagen vascular disorders). The condition can, however, appear for the first time up to one year after the last exposure.

When is health surveillance required?

311 Regulation 7 of the Control of Vibration at Work Regulations 2005 requires employers to provide suitable health surveillance where the risk assessment indicates a risk to employees' health. In any case, employees likely to be exposed in excess of the daily exposure action value of 2.5 m/s² $A(8)$ should be under suitable health surveillance.

312 Health surveillance should be instituted for:

- employees who are likely to be regularly exposed above the exposure action value;

- employees likely to be occasionally exposed above the exposure action value where the risk assessment identifies that the frequency and severity of exposure may pose a risk to health; and

- employees who have a diagnosis of HAVS (even when exposed below the exposure action value).

Competency and training

313 It is essential that health professionals involved in health surveillance for HAVS can demonstrate that they have the necessary expertise. Specialist training is required to carry out adequate clinical assessments and avoid misdiagnosing symptoms of HAVS.

314 The Faculty of Occupational Medicine has adopted a framework of competencies and a syllabus of approved training for health professionals involved in health surveillance for HAVS. These Faculty documents are reproduced in Appendix 6. The syllabus is designed to enable training providers to prepare health professionals for an examination leading to a qualification approved by the Faculty. Health professionals should have gained this qualification or have achieved an equivalent level of competence. They should also have more general

training in occupational health or occupational medicine, normally demonstrated by having a diploma certificate or degree in occupational health or diploma in occupational medicine or by being an associate or member of the Faculty of Occupational Medicine.

315 Following the introduction of the Vibration Regulations in 2005, there may be a short-term need for health surveillance for HAVS to be carried out by professionals who have not yet had the necessary specialist training. They should, however, possess general occupational health or medicine qualifications and be familiar with the contents of this guidance. It is recommended that they complete the specialist training at an early opportunity. If reasonably practicable, such individuals should make arrangements to be able to consult a person with specialist knowledge of HAVS for advice as necessary.

316 The Faculty syllabus includes relevant information on conducting a health surveillance programme for HAVS and on wider issues such as the legal background, understanding of routes of vibration exposure, pathophysiology and the appropriate management of the condition. It is anticipated that a range of academic and private institutions will provide training courses based on the Faculty's syllabus. All health professionals involved in health surveillance for HAVS are expected to maintain up-to-date knowledge of the subject.

The health surveillance programme

317 It is important to give appropriate information to employees and encourage their full co-operation. Occupational health professionals who are providing clinical assessment and overseeing the health surveillance programme can help employers explain the serious nature of the disease and the aims of health surveillance. There is a need to ensure that employees are aware that the results of their health surveillance, with respect to fitness for work, will be disclosed to their employer, but that no clinical information can be given to anyone else without their consent.

318 The aims of the health surveillance programme are primarily to safeguard the health of employees (including identifying and protecting individuals at increased risk), but also to check the long-term effectiveness of control measures. One of the specific aims is to prevent employees developing a degree of HAVS that is associated with disabling loss of hand function. Health surveillance for HAVS is appropriate where a risk assessment has shown the need (see Part 2) and it should operate alongside a programme of vibration risk control measures.

319 When cases of the occupational diseases, HAVS and carpal tunnel syndrome in association with vibration are diagnosed by a doctor, they should be reported by the employer in accordance with regulation 5 and Schedule 3 of the Reporting of Injuries, Diseases and Dangerous Occurrences Regulations (RIDDOR) 1995.

320 When health surveillance is required, it should be carried out annually. Both initial (or baseline) assessment and routine health surveillance are needed for HAVS. Early assessment of newly-exposed employees is recommended, as susceptible individuals can develop symptoms in six months or less. Exposed employees should receive information on why and how to detect and report symptoms of HAVS.

Medical records

321 A record-keeping system for holding results of medical examinations and reports of symptoms will be needed as part of the health surveillance programme.

These are confidential medical records relating to individuals. Employees should be informed of the confidential results of each assessment and of any implications of the findings, such as the likely effects of their continuing to work with vibration.

A tiered approach to health surveillance

322 To identify employees with symptoms that require further investigation, while avoiding unnecessary use of specialist resources, a tiered approach to health surveillance is recommended. Occupational health professionals experienced in the clinical assessment and diagnosis of HAVS are specialised and therefore they are a limited resource. To take this into account, most appointments with doctors or nurses are limited to cases where symptoms suggestive of HAVS have been reported. This tiered approach (Tiers 1-5) is described in paragraphs 326-345.

Roles of health professionals in the tiered approach

323 The qualified person is a specialised health professional, usually an occupational health nurse, competent to make enquiries about symptoms and to carry out clinical examinations for assessment of HAVS.

324 The doctor is a specialised health professional, usually an occupational physician, competent to carry out clinical examinations and diagnosis of HAVS. The doctor is responsible for formal diagnosis and fitness-for-work decisions.

325 For a description of the competency and training expected of these health professionals, see paragraphs 313-316.

Tier 1: Initial or baseline assessment

326 Health surveillance programmes need to include an initial assessment for any new or existing employee before they begin exposure to vibration. One reason for this is that a baseline should be available from which to judge the results of routine health surveillance. The baseline assessment forms Tier 1.

327 New employees, or those changing jobs, who will be exposed for the first time, should be given suitable information about the hazards of vibration (for example, the HSE pocket card INDG296(rev1) *Hand-arm vibration: Advice for employees*), preferably before they give information related to their medical status. This will help to alert the employee to the potential health consequences of failing to report symptoms of HAVS. Tier 1 also provides an opportunity to educate employees about measures under an employee's control that will help to reduce the risks from transmission of vibration.

328 As a minimum requirement, initial pre-exposure assessment can be carried out using a self-administered questionnaire that includes questions about the person's medical history which is to be returned in confidence to the health professionals (see Appendix 2). Employees with no symptoms suggestive of HAVS, or relevant medical history, should be considered fit for work with exposure to vibration. The qualified person or doctor will see those with possible symptoms of HAVS for further assessment. The doctor will then decide whether the person is fit to work with vibration exposure.

329 It is recommended that individuals who suffer from certain relevant vascular or neurological disorders affecting the hand or arm, eg Raynaud's disease and carpal tunnel syndrome, are not exposed to vibration at work. Initial assessment by questionnaire and, if necessary, clinical assessment by the qualified person and the doctor will identify these individuals.

Tier 2: Annual (screening) questionnaire

330 This should be repeated annually to form the routine health surveillance for employees who are at risk but have not reported any symptoms suggestive of HAVS. A simple questionnaire is used to form an initial assessment of potential health effects (see questionnaire in Appendix 3).

331 The questionnaire can be used as a self-administered tool to gather information. Ideally, employees should be given reminders about the nature of the symptoms and the need to report them. It is useful to have a responsible person appointed as part of the health surveillance programme to help communicate to the employees how the simple screening questionnaire operates. Such a person should be carefully selected to have experience of the working environment and be able to gain the confidence and co-operation of employees. They need not be qualified but should have received training from an occupational health professional. They should understand the health surveillance procedures and the importance of confidentiality. They should be able to describe symptoms of HAVS to employees but should not attempt to diagnose disease. If an employee discloses that they have symptoms, the responsible person should not make judgements about the cause of the symptoms.

332 Completed questionnaires may be processed by the responsible person as long as this is acceptable to employees. However, it may be appropriate to have the questionnaires sent directly to the occupational health service provider so that the responsible person and employer do not see the answers given by individual employees. If the employee indicates 'yes' to any of the questions on the form, this does not mean that HAVS has been identified. Instead, the employee should be referred to a specialised nurse (qualified person) or doctor as the 'yes' triggers entry into a more detailed clinical assessment process, described here under Tiers 3 and 4. In the absence of reported symptoms, there is no need for referral for further assessment but the questionnaire should be repeated at 12-month intervals. This means that many employees will not need to attend an appointment with a health professional.

333 If symptoms appear for the first time or progress, employees should be encouraged to report any symptoms and not to wait until the next time that screening is carried out. Any reporting of symptoms triggers the need for further assessment (Tiers 3-4). HSE recommends that after three years of reporting no symptoms the employee should be referred for a consultation with the qualified person to provide an opportunity to more fully explore any possible symptoms that the individual may have experienced without appreciating their full significance.

Tier 3: Assessment by qualified person

334 This should normally follow Tier 2 if symptoms are reported. The assessment should be conducted by the qualified person. The doctor may be involved in carrying out some or all of the assessment in Tier 3, according to the local arrangements made by the providers of health surveillance.

335 An administered clinical questionnaire that asks about relevant symptoms and a limited clinical examination are recommended. It is helpful to have a standardised questionnaire on which to record information about the individual's history of exposure to vibration at work, any significant leisure time exposure, current medication, symptomatology and the results of the clinical examination. Recommended content for this questionnaire is given in Appendix 4 and detailed guidance on the procedures is given in the section 'Clinical assessment for HAVS' (see paragraphs 355-393).

336 The clinical examination by the qualified person is not a full medical examination but a targeted assessment. Examination is directed at vascular and neurological function in the arm and hand; a number of specific tests may be appropriate. A limited musculoskeletal examination is also recommended. An assessment of grip strength and manual dexterity should be made, ideally using a dynamometer for grip strength and the Purdue pegboard or other means for manual dexterity. If relevant symptoms are reported or clinical effects found, diagnosis, described below, will be required. A presumptive diagnosis may be recorded in Tier 3, as the role of the occupational health nurse or qualified person develops, but formal diagnosis is made by a doctor in Tier 4.

Tier 4: Formal diagnosis

337 Formal diagnosis is made by the doctor. Formal diagnosis is required for certain actions including reporting by employers of cases under RIDDOR 1995 and fitness-for-work recommendations. Doctors can help considerably in the reporting process by using the precise description of the disease listed in the Regulations so that the employer will be able to identify immediately whether the case is reportable (see Appendix 1). The reported history of symptoms is the most useful diagnostic information. Additional standardised tests described in Tier 5 are an option. If these tests are conducted, the results will be considered by the doctor when arriving at a diagnosis of HAVS.

Tier 5: Use of standardised tests (Optional)

338 In addition to clinical findings from Tiers 3 and 4, standardised tests can be conducted at some sites or referral centres for an employee who has signs or symptoms of HAVS. This testing is aimed at providing a quantitative assessment, which is compared against 'normal' data. If such testing is obtained, the final diagnosis of HAVS still depends upon the judgement of the doctor and will need to take account of the reported symptoms.

339 This tier is not required as part of routine health surveillance provision for a workforce exposed to vibration. It is considered to be potentially useful for studying the progression of the disease.

340 Results from more than one of the following may be obtained:

Vascular tests

- Finger rewarming after cold provocation test (CPT).

- Finger systolic blood pressure test (FSBP).

341 These two standardised tests measure different parameters, although both tests use a cold challenge to the hands or fingers. The method in the FSBP test measures systolic blood pressure in the digital arteries, whereas finger rewarming times reflecting blood flow post cold challenge are measured in the CPT. The result from the CPT is more likely to be affected by a number of factors, including the emotional state of the individual, due to the relatively large influence of the sympathetic nervous system.

342 Some researchers using the standardised test methods are concerned about the repeatability of the CPT in control subjects, ie abnormal (positive) results can appear in repeat tests in individuals with no history of symptoms of Raynaud's disease or HAVS. Other reservations have been expressed about the robustness of the FSBP test. Currently there is no consensus among UK testing practitioners on a

vascular test that is sufficiently robust to be recommended for diagnosis of HAVS in an employee undergoing health surveillance.

Sensorineural tests

■   Vibrotactile perception threshold (VPT).

■   Thermal (temperature) perception threshold (TPT).

343   These tests are considered to be useful in evaluating changes in perception that relate to loss of function if the disease has progressed. They can be used as an important part of the fitness-for-work decision.

344   Details of the test methods can be found in HSE Contract Research Report CRR 197/98 *Standardised diagnostic methods for assessing components of the hand-arm vibration syndrome* by Lindsell and Griffin.[23] It should be noted that test conditions and methodology need to be carefully controlled.

345   Symptoms that may relate to carpal tunnel syndrome may need to be investigated by nerve conduction tests. This will usually follow referral to the patient's general practitioner.

Management of the affected employee, including fitness for work

346   Any employee diagnosed as suffering from HAVS will need to receive advice from the doctor about their medical condition and the likelihood of disease progression with continued exposure. The advice will vary according to the severity of the disease. HAVS is classified according to severity in stages (1-3) using the Stockholm Workshop scales (see Table 6 and paragraphs 385-393). Continuing exposure may be acceptable in early cases. Diagnosis of new cases of HAVS (stage 1) should result in appropriate steps being taken by the employer to review the risk assessment and ensure that exposures are reduced to as low a level as is reasonably practicable. If exposure is adequately controlled, it may be possible to prevent employees with HAVS stage 1 from progressing to HAVS stage 2 before they reach retirement age. Health surveillance monitoring for the individual may need to take place more frequently, depending on the advice of the doctor, if there is concern about progression of the disease. The clinical assessment questionnaire (Appendix 4) can be modified so that a shortened version is used for repeat assessments.

347   Even if the employee does not give consent for medical information to be disclosed to the employer, it is the responsibility of the doctor to advise the employer on whether the employee is fit for work with exposure to vibration. A recommendation may need to be made on safety grounds. For example, significant loss of grip strength might increase the risk of accidental injury to the employee or their co-employees. In most cases, the main reason for judging an employee to be unfit for work with vibration is to prevent further deterioration that could cause disability.

348   If an employee is diagnosed as having HAVS stage 2 (sensorineural or vascular) the aim is to prevent HAVS stage 3 developing because this is a more severe form of the disease associated with significant loss of function and disability. At the onset of symptoms of HAVS stage 2, there should be a reassessment of exposure conditions and close monitoring of the individual for any progression of symptoms, especially functional impairment. Detailed recording of reported symptoms will be important. The doctor should start to consider whether the employee is unfit to continue with exposure as soon as there is evidence that symptoms are progressing within HAVS stage 2.

349 One difficulty is that the tests of function used in the clinical assessment are not likely to give a clear indication of early functional loss. Stage 2 is broad, ranging from relatively minor symptoms to those with persistent loss of perception. Ideally, the employee will only be declared unfit when the disease has reached 'late' stage 2. Some optional standardised sensorineural tests (vibrotactile perception threshold and thermal perception threshold tests) were described in the 'Tier 5' section. If the doctor decides to use these standardised tests, the results can be used to help assess the severity of the HAVS in stage 2 to help the decision on whether 'late' stage 2 has been reached.

350 A method for dividing HAVS stage 2 into 'early' and 'late' forms using these results from two sensorineural tests and an assessment of vascular symptoms will be described in the section on classification of symptoms (paragraphs 385-393). Dividing sensorineural HAVS stage 2 in the absence of the standardised test results relies upon categorising numbness/tingling symptoms as 'intermittent' or 'persistent'. This will be less effective. Progression to the 'late' form of stage 2 is a strong indicator of the employee being unfit for work with vibration. However, the available methods for assessment and prediction of progression are not necessarily precise, therefore the decision to advise the employer that an employee is unfit for work with vibration involves a significant element of clinical judgement.

351 Management of existing cases of HAVS stage 2 and stage 3 is potentially different as more information may be available about the rate of progression over time. An older employee, close to retirement age, with no indication of recent rapid progression of symptoms, and who fully understands the risks involved in ongoing exposures, may be allowed to continue work with limited exposure under regular health surveillance.

352 If carpal tunnel syndrome is diagnosed, the employee may need to be removed from exposure to vibration. Where a non-occupational condition is suspected, the employee should be referred to their general practitioner. Outcome of surgical decompression in carpal tunnel syndrome can be less favourable in HAVS patients than in people with no history of vibration exposure. Recommendations for return to work with exposure to vibration should be made on an individual basis and the employee should be informed of the possible return of symptoms with continued exposure.

353 When a recommendation is made by the doctor that an employee is no longer fit for exposure to vibration, the employer has to decide on the appropriate action to take. Factors such as the scope for further reductions in exposure and availability of other work with no exposure to vibration may play a part in this decision-making process. For the employee, there may be several obstacles to getting another job which does not involve exposure to vibration. These might include the need to acquire additional training and skills, economic, social and cultural factors and an inability to work outdoors.

354 In addition to the requirement to supply individual fitness data, anonymised grouped results of health surveillance should, where practicable, be divulged to the employer by the occupational health professional and be used as a basis to assess the adequacy of vibration risk controls. In the case of large groups, individual consent is not required for this and the data should be given to the employer, but where the group of employees is small, confidentiality will have to be addressed. If standardised test results are obtained (see 'Tier 5' section), these may be useful in monitoring any changes in the severity of HAVS in groups of employees.

Clinical assessment for HAVS

355 This section covers many of the details of how to carry out a clinical assessment for HAVS and will help the occupational health professional when completing the recommended clinical questionnaire in Appendix 4. The process of assessment relates to Tiers 3-4 and is normally carried out by an occupational health nurse and occupational physician.

356 A comfortable or warm room temperature, preferably without wide variations in temperature, is recommended for the clinical examination. The individual's history of symptoms and any relationship with the person's work needs to be recorded. The questionnaire contains a free text area to record responses at the start of the interview. Open questions such as 'Do you have problems with your hands?' might be asked while leading questions need to be avoided to allow the individual to explain in their own words.

Hand symptoms

357 Symptoms of HAVS were described in the earlier section 'Clinical effects' but some additional information is given here.

358 Tingling and numbness may occur as part of a normal physiological response to the use of vibrating tools. If this response lasts more than 20 minutes it is more likely to be part of a pathological process. Numbness is also associated with vasospasm. Numbness occurring separately from blanching is of prime interest as this may indicate the neurological component of HAVS. Tingling in HAVS is usually worsened by cold exposure. Symptoms of tingling or numbness in the fingers at night or on arm elevation may indicate carpal tunnel syndrome. The latter is a peripheral nerve disorder that can be caused by exposure to vibration. It is characterised by:

- median nerve distribution of tingling and pain;

- being woken at night by hand symptoms such as pain or numbness;

- pains in the wrist radiating into the forearm;

- median nerve distribution of blunting of sensation;

- positive Tinel and Phalen's tests (see 'Examination' paragraphs 379-384);

- wasting of abductor pollicis brevis in more severe long-standing cases.

359 Subjects may volunteer that certain actions such as flicking or shaking the hands relieves symptoms of carpal tunnel syndrome. More diffuse symptoms of tingling and a complaint of a weak grip would tend to favour HAVS. (A weak grip is not normally a feature of carpal tunnel syndrome until the condition is well advanced.)

360 There should be sufficient detailed description of the attacks of blanching to differentiate between abnormal arterial vasospasm (sometimes known as Raynaud's phenomenon) and a normal physiological response to cold. Vasospasm that reflects the vascular component of HAVS causes whiteness initially affecting the tips of the digits and then extending proximally to the palm. The whiteness is usually circumferential and there will be a 'sharp' line of demarcation between normal and abnormal skin colour. Blotchiness or diffuse paleness of the skin is not what is meant by blanching in this context. Whiteness is often but not always followed by blueness and redness due to the hyperaemic phase.

361 Blanching attacks are more likely to occur in the winter months because cold is the main trigger. 'Attacks' lasting many hours or days are not related to abnormal vasospasm since the latter are known to last about 20-60 minutes. 'At other times?' on the questionnaire might refer, for example, to emotion acting as a trigger. Whiteness in the toes/feet is more likely to indicate primary Raynaud's phenomenon (Raynaud's disease) although there is a possibility that exposure to vibration can affect non-exposed extremities in HAVS cases where fingers blanch. Blanching with a more diffuse demarcation of whiteness in a distinct ulnar distribution may indicate the relatively rare hypothenar hammer syndrome and should be investigated further for possible treatment. This syndrome is usually associated with specific work activities or tool use. Blanching due to HAVS may only rarely be witnessed by the occupational health professional. It is unethical to actively attempt to trigger an attack by cooling the hands and, in any case, such attempts are often not successful. It may be useful to show a photograph of a typical example of an attack of blanching to the employee.

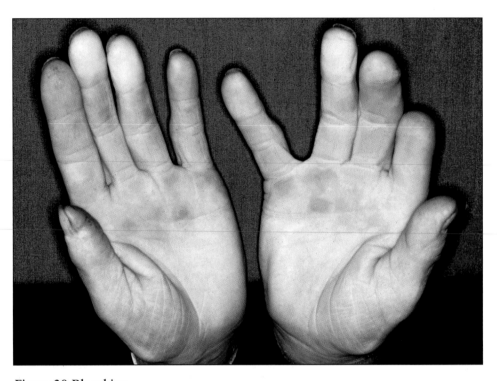

Figure 20 Blanching

362 Difficulties may be experienced for example when fastening buttons or manipulating small objects which may result from areas of reduced sensitivity in an individual suffering from the neurological component of HAVS. It is important to ascertain if this is during attacks of blanching or if it occurs when the fingers are warm and the person is in a warm environment. The individual should be asked about the type of activities interfered with, the type of problem and whether interference only occurs in cold weather or continues throughout the year.

363 Musculoskeletal symptoms in the upper limb may be caused by risk factors such as working posture and not vibration *per se*, or by a combination of vibration exposure and handling heavy tools while applying a large grip force.

Occupational history

364 The leading hand is the hand nearest to the source of vibration, if this can be identified. It should not be assumed that this hand will be more badly affected as

cases will vary and depend on the variety of jobs, hand positions and tools used. All activities involving exposure to vibration are relevant. The 'trigger' or contact time is the estimated time for which the hands are actually exposed to vibration. This will often be considerably shorter than the period during which the tool is said to be used (see Part 2).

365 Some chemical agents are neurotoxic and may cause neurological symptoms similar to those of HAVS. Those encountered in the workplace may include:

- acrylamide;

- antimony;

- arsenic;

- carbon disulphide;

- diethyl thiocarbamate;

- lead (inorganic);

- mercury compounds;

- methylbutyl ketone;

- n-hexane;

- some organophosphates;

- thallium;

- TOCP.

Social history/leisure pursuits

366 Use of motorcycles should be included in leisure activities. Sources of vibration exposure and approximate 'trigger' times need to be recorded. Occasional use of DIY tools is not likely to be relevant.

Medical history

367 Any injuries or surgery to the hand, arm or neck will need to be considered as part of the clinical assessment.

368 Vascular symptoms of HAVS (Raynaud's phenomenon) may arise spontaneously in the general population from a variety of causes including Raynaud's disease (primary Raynaud's phenomenon) which affects about 3% of men and about 10% of women. As part of differential diagnosis of HAVS, it is appropriate to address whether there is reasonable certainty that the person does not have Raynaud's disease. Factors in favour of Raynaud's disease include:

- early age of onset (teens or twenties);

- usually a description of other cold extremities (ears, feet, nose);

- a symmetrical pattern of blanching;

- family history.

369 Raynaud's phenomenon other than primary Raynaud's is known as 'secondary' Raynaud's phenomenon. A number of other conditions are listed below that lead to a tendency to report similar vascular symptoms to those of HAVS, ie secondary Raynaud's phenomenon. In fact, many of these conditions are associated with a complaint of cold extremities and do not cause arterial vasospasm. It may be difficult to separate the symptoms which might arise from the effects of ageing on skin blood flow from those which may arise from HAVS. The list of conditions is not exhaustive:

- atherosclerosis;

- cervical rib;

- CREST syndrome;

- dermatomyositis;

- hyperfibrinogenaemia;

- hypothyroidism;

- leukaemia;

- polyarteritis nodosa;

- polycythaemia rubra vera;

- rheumatoid arthritis;

- scleroderma;

- systemic lupus erythematosus;

- the presence of cold haemagglutinins;

- thoracic outlet syndrome;

- thrombo-embolic disease;

- vasculitis;

- vasculopathy in diabetes.

370 A few drug treatments and toxins are associated with symptoms of secondary Raynaud's phenomenon:

- beta blockers;

- bleomycin;

- ergot;

- methysergide;

- vinblastine;

- vinyl chloride.

371 The symptoms attributed to the neurological component of HAVS may arise from some medical conditions. These include:

■ alcoholic peripheral neuropathy;

■ carpal tunnel syndrome (see paragraphs 358-359);

■ cervical spondylosis (where one root is affected on one side);

■ diabetic peripheral neuropathy;

■ hemiplegia;

■ multiple sclerosis;

■ neurofibromatosis;

■ poliomyelitis;

■ spinal cord compression;

■ syringomyelia.

372 Drug treatment can sometimes cause neuropathy. For example:

■ chloramphenicol;

■ cyclosporine;

■ ethambutol;

■ gold;

■ indomethacin;

■ isoniazid;

■ metronidazole;

■ nitrofurantoin;

■ perhexiline;

■ phenytoin;

■ polymyxin;

■ streptomycin;

■ vincristine.

373 In addition, a number of chemicals in the workplace can cause peripheral neuropathy (see 'Occupational history' paragraphs 364-365).

Examination

374 A limited clinical examination is carried out to include the items mentioned on the clinical questionnaire form (see Appendix 4).

375 If a neuropathy is suspected from an examination of the hands and/or medical history, an examination of the feet is necessary and a check for an autonomic neuropathy should be made. If pulse or blood pressure is reduced in either arm, evidence of a subclavian bruit should be sought.

376 Allen's test examines the patency of the palmar arches and digital arteries. Normal anatomical variations may give rise to false positive results in this test. The examiner, standing, uses the fingers of each hand to compress the radial and ulnar arteries at the wrist and then raises the subject's hand while the subject opens and closes the hand to empty the palmar arches and subcutaneous vessels. The hand is then lowered and one of the arteries released. Prompt flushing of the hand indicates a normal contribution from the tested artery. Faint and delayed flushing of the fingers indicates that either the deep palmar or the digital arteries are occluded. A delay of more than five seconds indicates digital artery occlusion.

377 Light touch can be elicited using cotton wool and superficial pain using a sterile pin or broken orange stick but the high inter-observer error makes these procedures of little value in practice and they are not recommended. Monofilaments, such as Semmes-Weinstein monofilaments, can be used to test perception of light touch and deep pressure. The testing kit consists of probes of varying thickness of nylon, which are presented to the subject until the probe deforms at a defined force. Recognition is recorded in a standardised way and the test should be performed with the subject having no visual clues to the application of the monofilaments.

378 The Purdue pegboard can be used to help assess manipulative dexterity and tactile sensibility. The test instructions should be followed and an assessment made separately for each hand. An alternative system, the nine-hole peg test, can also be used but is likely to give less adequate information. Both systems have normative data available. If these tests are not available, qualitative assessment can be made using a selection of small coins, washers or bolts. Deficit in manual dexterity associated with **severe** cases of the neurological component of HAVS is usually evident during medical interview in the manner in which the subject handles pieces of paper, uses a pen and grasps and turns door handles.

379 Adson's, Tinel's and Phalen's tests are available for use where appropriate.

380 Adson's test is only necessary where the history of positional symptoms points to thoracic outlet syndrome. During deep inspiration, with the head rotated to the side being tested and the arm abducted, the radial artery at the wrist is palpated. In the presence of subclavian obstruction, the radial pulse is reduced or absent. The false positive rate is about 10%.

381 Tinel's and Phalen's tests are used to elicit symptoms indicative of carpal tunnel syndrome and are therefore appropriate to use when the subject complains of tingling in the fingers in the median distribution. For a description of carpal tunnel syndrome see paragraphs 358-359 in the earlier section on 'Hand symptoms'. For Tinel's test, the subject's hand and forearm are rested horizontally on a flat, firm surface with the palm uppermost. The examiner places his/her index finger over the carpal tunnel at the wrist and applies a sharp tap to it with a tendon hammer. A complaint of tingling in the subject's fingers in the median nerve distribution is indicative of carpal tunnel syndrome. In Phalen's test, the

subject raises his/her arms to chin level and then allows both hands to flex at the wrist by gravity. This posture should be maintained for three minutes. Tingling in the fingers in the median nerve distribution is indicative of compression of the median nerve under the carpal ligament.

382 Grip strength should be tested using a dynamometer. A standard handle position is usually used for each test. Standardised protocols have employed:

■   the subject seated, shoulder adducted, neutral rotation, elbow flexed at 90 degrees and the arm unsupported;

■   standing while lowering the arm from the outstretched horizontal position, ensuring that the dynamometer does not touch the thigh.

383 The average result from three attempts in each hand should be recorded.

384 The final page in the questionnaire gives space to record the overall results of the assessment. The Stockholm Workshop scales should be used to classify vascular and sensorineural symptoms. Results from any further investigations can be recorded on the form. It may be appropriate to obtain further test results from standardised methods (see paragraphs 338-345) and to divide any stage 2 cases of HAVS into 'early' and 'late' (see paragraphs 385-393). For details on how to make a recommendation on fitness for work, see paragraphs 346-354.

Classification of symptoms using the Stockholm Workshop scales and methods for dividing stage 2

385 The classification scheme known as the Stockholm Workshop scales should be used to classify neurological and vascular symptoms (see Table 6). One disadvantage of the scales is the lack of precise definition for some of the terms used (eg 'frequent').

Table 6 Stockholm Workshop scales

Vascular component		
Stage	*Grade*	*Description*
0		No attacks
1_V	Mild	Occasional attacks affecting only the tips of one or more fingers
2_V	Moderate	Occasional attacks affecting distal and middle (rarely also proximal) phalanges of one or more fingers
3_V	Severe	Frequent attacks affecting all phalanges of most fingers
4_V	Very severe	As in stage 3, with trophic changes in the fingertips

Sensorineural component	
Stage	Description
0$_{SN}$	Vibration-exposed but no symptoms
1$_{SN}$	Intermittent numbness with or without tingling
2$_{SN}$	Intermittent or persistent numbness, reduced sensory perception
3$_{SN}$	Intermittent or persistent numbness, reduced tactile discrimination and/or manipulative dexterity

Note: *The staging is made separately for each hand. The grade of disorder is indicated by the stage and number of affected fingers on both hands, eg stage/hand/number of digits.*

386 A system for allocating a weighted numerical value to each phalange affected and calculating an overall score for finger blanching in each hand is used in the Griffin method (Figure 21).[24] This system is a useful method in practice for monitoring progression or regression of symptoms in individual fingers. It does not take account of the frequency of attacks, which may be more relevant in assessing functional disability. Some attacks can lead to a variable degree of blanching. In this case the worst distribution should be recorded.

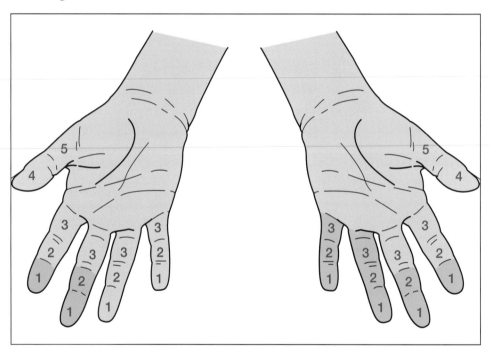

Figure 21 Numerical scoring of vascular symptoms of HAVS

387 In the numerical scoring system for vascular HAVS, the blanching for each part of each digit is given a score as indicated on the diagram in Figure 21. A total value for each hand can be arrived at by summing the digit scores. In the figure, the score for the left hand is 16 and that for the right hand is 4.

388 If an employee is diagnosed as having stage 2, the aim is to prevent stage 3 (vascular or sensorineural) developing because this is a more severe form of the disease associated with significant loss of function and disability (see paragraphs 346-354). Stage 2 sensorineural is broad, ranging from minor neurological symptoms to those with persistent sensorineural loss. Therefore stage 2 should be divided into 'early' and 'late' phases to assist with management of stage 2 cases.

389 Lawson and McGeoch have published a method of adapting the Stockholm workshop classification scheme to divide stage 2.[25] They have used the sum of the scores from two standardised sensorineural tests to divide the sensorineural stage 2 into 'early' and 'late'. The standardised tests are described in paragraphs 338-345. The scores relating to the vibrotactile perception threshold and thermal perception threshold tests are derived using the scheme given in Table 7. Numbness and tingling are given equal weighting in this adaptation.

Table 7 Scoring system for the standardised tests

Vibrotactile threshold test (index and little finger)			
At 31.4 Hz	< 0.3 ms^2 = 0	≥ 0.3 ms^2, < 0.4 ms^2 = 1	≥ 0.4 ms^2 = 2
At 125 Hz	< 0.7 ms^2 = 0	≥ 0.7 ms^2, < 1.0 ms^2 = 1	≥ 1.0 ms^2 = 2
Thermal perception threshold test (1°/second, index and little finger)			
Temperature neutral zone	$< 21°C$ = 0	$\geq 21°C$, $< 27°C$ = 2	$\geq 27°C$ = 4

390 Reduced sensory perception can be assessed by the use of Semmes-Weinstein monofilaments and reduced manual dexterity by the Purdue pegboard as described in the 'Clinical assessment for HAVS' section. If a loss of dexterity in a warm environment is diagnosed, and the total score for the two sensorineural tests is 9 or higher, then a score of 10 is added to this result but only if the Purdue pegboard result is abnormal. Hence the scoring criteria for stage 3 sensorineural is 19 or above in Table 8. The terms 'intermittent', 'persistent' and 'constant' (as defined by Dr Ian Lawson) help differentiate between stage 2 'early' and 'late' and stage 3 (see Table 8).

391 If no standardised test results are obtained, the process of dividing stage 2 sensorineural relies upon whether symptoms of numbness/tingling are intermittent or persistent, and will be less effective as a consequence.

392 To separate 'early' and 'late' stage 2 vascular, the terms 'occasional' and 'frequent' are used in Table 8 (as defined by Dr Ian Lawson) and Griffin blanching scores are used.

393 It should be realised that this scheme is indicative. In some individual cases, occupational health professionals may need to use their professional judgement to allocate the individual to 'early' or 'late' stage 2.

Table 8 Guide to sensorineural and vascular staging

Sensorineural

STAGE	CRITERIA	ASSESSMENT	
		Left Hand	Right Hand
0_{SN}	Vibration exposure but no symptoms		
1_{SN}	Intermittent numbness and/or tingling (with a sensorineural, SN, score of > 3 and < 6)		
2_{SN} (early)	Intermittent numbness, and/or tingling, reduced sensory perception (usually an SN score of $\geq 6 < 9$)		
2_{SN} (late)	Persistent numbness, and/or tingling, reduced sensory perception (usually an SN score of $\geq 9 \leq 16$)		
3_{SN}	Constant numbness and/or tingling, reduced sensory perception and manipulative dexterity in warmth (and an SN score ≥ 19)		

Vascular

STAGE	CRITERIA	ASSESSMENT	
		Left Hand	Right Hand
0_V	No attacks		
1_V	Attacks affecting only the tips of the distal phalanges of one or more fingers (usually a blanching score of 1-4)		
2_V (early)	Occasional attacks of whiteness affecting the distal and middle (rarely also the proximal) phalanges of one or more fingers (usually a blanching score of 5-9)		
2_V (late)	Frequent attacks of whiteness affecting the distal and middle (rarely also proximal) phalanges of one or more fingers (usually a blanching score of 10-16)		
3_V	Frequent attacks of whiteness affecting all of the phalanges of most of the fingers all year (usually a blanching score of 18 or more)		
4_V	As 3V and trophic changes		

Definitions
Intermittent - not persistent
Persistent - lasting > than 2 hours
Constant - present all of the time
Occasional - 3 or < attacks per week
Frequent - > 3 attacks per week

Treatment

Therapeutic interventions

394 Therapeutic interventions for HAVS are of limited benefit. Those suffering from HAVS are advised to keep their hands, feet and body warm by reducing their exposure to cold and wearing appropriate clothing. This may include weatherproof clothing, headwear and insulated gloves and boots. The use of chemical heat packs in gloves or boots, breaks taken in a warm environment and the use of hand driers blowing warm air on the hands during breaks are likely to be beneficial. Some benefit may be obtained by stopping smoking. Reducing noise exposure might also help to reduce the frequency of blanching.

Pharmaceutical agents for the treatment of HAVS

395 The evidence for the effectiveness of pharmaceutical agents in the treatment of the vascular symptoms of HAVS is limited. No studies showing long-term benefits have been published, and much of the evidence is based upon treatment given for the vascular symptoms when these arise from causes other than vibration (eg Raynaud's disease).

396 Calcium antagonists, alpha-adreno receptor antagonists, antifibrinolytics and prostenoids have all been used to treat the vascular symptoms of HAVS. However, a beneficial response is commonly associated with significant side effects. The most commonly used drug is Nifedipine: patients may find the side effects of ankle swelling, headaches and blushing unacceptable, although these may be reduced by using modified release preparations. Prostaglandin analogues have also been used, but this usually requires in-patient stay for several days to receive intravenous infusions. Significant side-effects, including hypotension, may restrict the dose given, which may reduce the effectiveness of the drug. Any improvement in symptoms is normally temporary. In general, the use of prostaglandin analogues is not appropriate.

397 No pharmaceutical treatment is available for the neurological component of HAVS.

Surgical interventions for HAVS

398 Sympathectomy, in one of its forms, has been used to treat Raynaud's disease. Usually a major improvement in symptoms can be achieved but only for a limited period of time. Sympathectomy for Raynaud's disease is best reserved for those individuals who appear to be heading towards irreversible digital gangrene, in whom it may delay the progression of the disease. Operative sympathectomy for Raynaud's phenomenon in HAVS can rarely, if ever, be justified. Digital sympathectomy has rarely been employed in patients with vasospastic symptoms of HAVS. The technique does receive limited support in the surgical literature for providing some benefit to patients with chronic digital ischaemia although the benefit is temporary in many cases. Many patients studied have had progressive collagen vascular disease. The technique has not been assessed on an isolated group of patients having vibration-induced vasospasm. This therapeutic approach cannot currently be justified in patients with circulatory problems arising from HAVS. Sympathectomy in the hand can be achieved pharmacologically by using a regional block. However, this is temporary in its effect and it probably has no application to HAVS.

399 Overall, the role of a sympathectomy in Raynaud's disease is extremely limited and in HAVS there can be very few occasions, if any, when its use is justified.

The management of carpal tunnel syndrome in association with HAVS

400 There is considered to be an approximate doubling of risk of carpal tunnel syndrome in people exposed to vibration. A patient's history may be consistent with the neurological component of HAVS and also carpal tunnel syndrome. Surgical decompression of the carpal tunnel in such circumstances has been shown to be an effective intervention in relieving symptoms of carpal tunnel syndrome. Carpal tunnel decompression in patients not exposed to vibration, generally produces a very favourable outcome. The results of carpal tunnel decompression in those suffering from HAVS is probably less satisfactory, but still worthwhile.

Acknowledgement
HSE acknowledges the contribution of the Working Group on Hand-transmitted Vibration of the Faculty of Occupational Medicine of the Royal College of Physicians and the Medical Assessment Process of the Department of Trade and Industry.

Appendix 1

Reportable diseases

1   The Reporting of Injuries, Diseases and Dangerous Occurrences Regulations 1995 (RIDDOR) require employers to report cases of ill health associated with exposure to hand-arm vibration, as set out below.

2   Carpal tunnel syndrome is reportable for all work involving hand-held vibrating tools, while hand-arm vibration syndrome is reportable for the work activities listed.

The Reporting of Injuries, Diseases and Dangerous Occurrences Regulations 1995 Extracts from Schedule 3, Part I: Occupational diseases	
Column 1	*Column 2*
Diseases	*Activities*
13. Carpal tunnel syndrome	Work involving the use of hand-held vibrating tools.
14. Hand-arm vibration syndrome	Work involving: (a) the use of chain saws, brush cutters or hand-held or hand-fed circular saws in forestry or woodworking; (b) the use of hand-held rotary tools in grinding material or in sanding or polishing metal; (c) the holding of material being ground or metal being sanded or polished by rotary tools; (d) the use of hand-held percussive metal-working tools or the holding of metal being worked upon by percussive tools in connection with riveting, caulking, chipping, hammering, fettling or swaging; (e) the use of hand-held powered percussive drills or hand-held powered percussive hammers in mining, quarrying or demolition, or on roads or footpaths (including road construction); or (f) the holding of material being worked upon by pounding machines in shoe manufacture.

Initial screening questionnaire

MEDICAL IN CONFIDENCE

INITIAL SCREENING QUESTIONNAIRE FOR WORKERS USING HAND-HELD VIBRATING TOOLS, HAND-GUIDED VIBRATING MACHINES AND HAND-FED VIBRATING MACHINES

Date:...

Employee name:..

Occupation:...

Address:..

Date of birth:..

National Insurance no:..

Employer name:..

Have you ever used hand-held vibrating tools, machines or hand-fed processes in your job?   Y/N

If YES:
(a) list year of first exposure...

(b) when was the last time you used them?...
(detail work history overleaf)

1 Do you have any tingling of the fingers lasting more than 20 minutes after using vibrating equipment?   Y/N

2 Do you have tingling of the fingers at any other time?   Y/N

3 Do you wake at night with pain, tingling, or numbness in your hand or wrist?   Y/N

4 Do one or more of your fingers go numb more than 20 minutes after using vibrating equipment?   Y/N

5 Have your fingers gone white* on cold exposure?   Y/N

Whiteness means a clear discoloration of the fingers with a sharp edge, usually followed by a red flush.

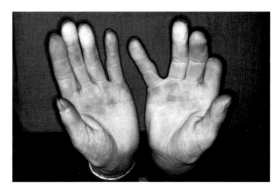

Blanching

6 If Yes to 5, do you have difficulty rewarming them when leaving the cold? Y/N

7 Do your fingers go white at any other time? Y/N

8 Are you experiencing any other problems with the muscles or joints of the hands or arms? Y/N

9 Do you have difficulty picking up very small objects, eg screws or buttons or opening tight jars? Y/N

10 Have you ever had a neck, arm or hand injury or operation? Y/N

If so give details...

11 Have you ever had any serious diseases of joints, skin, nerves, heart or blood vessels? Y/N

If so give details...

12 Are you on any long-term medication? Y/N

If so give details...

OCCUPATIONAL HISTORY

Dates   Job Title

....
....
....
....
....
....
....
....
....

I certify that all the answers given above are true to the best of my knowledge and belief.

Signed: Date:

RETURN IN CONFIDENCE TO:

....

Annual screening questionnaire for health surveillance

SCREENING QUESTIONNAIRE FOR WORKERS USING HAND-HELD VIBRATING TOOLS, HAND-GUIDED VIBRATING MACHINES AND HAND-FED VIBRATING MACHINES

Date:...

Employee name:...

Occupation:..

Address:..

Date of birth:...

National Insurance no:...

Employer name:..

Date of previous screening:...

Have you been using hand-held vibrating tools, machines or hand-fed   Y/N
processes in your job, or if this is a review, since your last assessment?
(detail work history overleaf)

If NO or more than 2 years since last exposure please return the form - there is no need to answer further questions.

If YES:

1 Do you have any numbness or tingling of the fingers lasting more than   Y/N
20 minutes after using vibrating equipment?

2 Do you have numbness or tingling of the fingers at any other time?   Y/N

3 Do you wake at night with pain, tingling, or numbness in your hand   Y/N
or wrist?

4 Have any of your fingers gone white* on cold exposure?   Y/N

Whiteness means a clear discoloration of the fingers with a sharp edge, usually followed by a red flush.

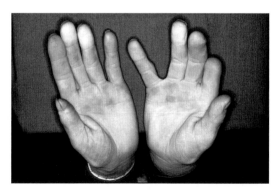

Blanching

5 Have you noticed any change in your response to your tolerance of working outdoors in the cold?   Y/N

6 Are you experiencing any other problems in your hands or arms?   Y/N

7 Do you have difficulty picking up very small objects, eg screws or buttons or opening tight jars?   Y/N

8 Has anything changed about your health since the last assessment ?   Y/N

I certify that all the answers given above are true to the best of my knowledge and belief.

Signed: Date:

RETURN TO:

Hand-arm vibration syndrome (HAVS):

- is a disorder which affects the blood vessels, nerves, muscles and joints of the hand, wrist and arm;

- can become severely disabling if ignored; and

- its best known form is vibration white finger (VWF) which can be triggered by cold or wet weather and can cause severe pain in the affected fingers.

Signs to look out for in hand-arm vibration syndrome:

- tingling and numbness in the fingers;

- in the cold and wet, fingers go white, then blue, then red and are painful;

- you can't feel things with your fingers;

- pain, tingling or numbness in your hands, wrists and arms;

- loss of strength in hands.

OCCUPATIONAL HISTORY

Dates   Job Title

....
....
....
....
....
....
....
....
....

Clinical questionnaire

MEDICAL IN CONFIDENCE
HEALTH SURVEILLANCE QUESTIONNAIRE

ASSESSMENT OF HAND-ARM VIBRATION SYNDROME

Date:

Mr/Mrs/Miss/Ms SURNAME ....FORENAMES ....

ADDRESS..

.... POST CODE ....

DATE OF BIRTH

ETHNIC GROUP:

European   Afro Caribbean   Asian   Other

OCCUPATION .... EMPLOYER ....

GENERAL PRACTITIONER ADDRESS...

....

Free text area to ask general questions about the person's work and symptoms

HAND SYMPTOMS

Blanching

	Yes	No
Have you ever suffered from your fingers going white?		

If No go to the section on Tingling symptoms.

If yes (and still occurring in the last 2 years) does it occur:

	Yes	No
In response to cold, damp or wet conditions?		
While working?		
At other times?		

Please give examples

....

....

....

....

....

When did you first notice this whiteness?   Year ....

How often does it occur?	Yes	No
Several times a year		
Several times a month		
Several times a day		
Every day		
Does it occur in winter only		
Winter and summer		

State most common circumstances

....

....

	Yes	No
Do you experience whiteness in your feet or other periphery?		

If yes state where...

Which fingers are affected? (shade all parts that have ever gone white)

Right hand   **Left hand**

Witnessed [ ] Not witnessed [ ] by person completing screening

Tingling (excluding transient tingling lasting for up to 20 minutes after using vibrating tools)

Do you have tingling of the fingers?	Yes	No
In response to cold?		
With blanching?		
While working?		
At other times?		

If other times, what circumstances, and how long does it last?

....

....

....

When did you first notice this?...Year ....

Which fingers are affected? (shade all affected parts)

Right hand   **Left hand**

Numbness (excluding transient tingling lasting for up to 20 minutes after using vibrating tools)

Do your fingers go numb?	Yes	No
In response to cold?		
With blanching?		
While working?		
At other times?		

If other times, what circumstances, and how long does it last?

....

....

....

When did you first notice this?...Year ....

Right hand   **Left hand**

	Yes	No
Do you have any difficulty handling or manipulating small objects?		

If yes when does this occur?...

	Yes	No
Do any of these symptoms (blanching, tingling or numbness) affect your work or leisure activities?		

If yes, give details

....

....

Musculoskeletal

	Yes	No
Are you experiencing problems with the muscles or joints of your hands/arms/wrists/elbows/shoulders?		

	Yes	No
Pain		
Stiffness		
Swelling		
Weakness		

If yes, give details

....

....

OCCUPATIONAL HISTORY

Right handed ☐ Left handed ☐ Leading hand: Right ☐ Left ☐

When did you first start using vibrating tools or equipment?................................

Where do you notice the vibration most? ....

If you no longer use vibrating tools when did you stop?...........................

Which of the main elements of your present job involve use of vibrating tools or equipment and how much time per day ('trigger' or contact time)?

	Hours/Day	Days/Week
(a)		
(b)		
(c)		
(d)		

When did you join the company? ....

List main jobs and departments in order: Hours/Day   Years

(a) .... ☐ ☐

(b) .... ☐ ☐

(c) .... ☐ ☐

(d) .... ☐ ☐

What jobs did you do previously, outside this company, involving vibration?

(a) .... ☐ ☐

(b) .... ☐ ☐

(c) .... ☐ ☐

(d) .... ☐ ☐

                                                          Yes   No

Have you had any exposure to chemicals at work? ☐☐

If yes, give details

....

....

SOCIAL HISTORY/ LEISURE PURSUITS
                                                          Yes   No

Do any of your hobbies expose you to hand-arm ☐☐
vibration?

If yes, give details

....

....

Are you a smoker? ☐   Non-smoker? ☐   Ex-smoker? ☐

If smoker, how many do you smoke each day? ..../day

If ex-smoker, when did you stop? ....

Do you drink alcohol?

If yes, how many units per week? ....units/week

MEDICAL HISTORY

	Yes	No
Do other members of your family suffer from white finger? (brothers, sisters and parents only)		

If so, who? ....

	Yes	No
Have you ever had a neck/arm/hand injury or operation?		

If so, what and when? ....

	Yes	No
Were you left with any problems?		

If so, what? ....

Have you ever had any serious disease of:

	Yes	No
Joints?		
Skin?		
Nerves?		
Heart or blood vessels?		
Other?		

If so, give details

....

....

	Yes	No
Are you on any long-term medication or treatment for any condition:		

If so, give details?

....

....

EXAMINATION

(Note last exposure to vibration)   Room temperature °C

Appearance of hands Note any signs of vascular disease, deformity, scars, callosities or muscle wasting.

Right hand   **Left hand**

Circulation

Pulse rate (bpm)   Blood pressure (mm Hg)
Lying/sitting

Right [   ]   Right [   ]
Left [   ]   Left [   ]

		Present	Absent			Present	Absent
Radial pulse	Rt			Lt			
Ulnar pulse	Rt			Lt			

		Positive	Negative			Positive	Negative
Allen's test	Rt			Lt			

Nervous System

		Normal	Abnormal			Normal	Abnormal
Semmes-Weinstein	Rt			Lt			
Manual dexterity	Rt			Lt			
(Purdue Pegboard test)							

Further tests, where appropriate

Adson's test	Rt			Lt			
Tinel's test	Rt			Lt			
Phalen's test	Rt			Lt			

Musculoskeletal

Describe any abnormality of neck or upper limbs ....

....

	Rt	Lt

Grip strength   [   ] [   ] [   ]   [   ] [   ] [   ]
(in kg)

Average   [   ]

ASSESSMENT OF HISTORY AND EXAMINATION

Vascular

	Yes	No
Primary Raynaud's phenomenon present?		
Secondary Raynaud's phenomenon present?		
If so, is this vibration induced?		

	Right	Left
Stockholm Vascular grading		

Neurological

Neurological impairment suggested by clinical assessment?

	Right	Left
Stockholm Sensorineural grading		

	Yes	No
Is carpal tunnel syndrome suggested by history and findings?		

Musculoskeletal

	Yes	No
Muscular or soft tissue disorder present?		
Evidence of skeletal disorder		

Latent periods

	Years
Vascular	
Neurological	
Musculoskeletal	

	Yes	No
Further special investigations required?		

Results

Vibrotactile Threshold   Rt   Lt

Temperature Threshold   Rt   Lt

	Yes	No
Fit for work with exposure to hand-transmitted vibration?		

Any conditions or vibration restrictions to be followed?..

....

....

	Yes	No
Has advisory leaflet been received by employee?		

Comments on overall assessment

....

....

Date for next medical review..

Signature: ....
Nursing/Medical Officer

Training and competence issues for those advising employers

1   The Vibration Regulations require employers to make a 'suitable and sufficient' assessment of the risks arising from vibration. For many employers this will be a straightforward process and they will be able to understand and follow the guidance in Part 2 of this book without professional help. Some employers may need to appoint one or more of their employees to undertake these tasks, while others will wish to employ external assistance to help them with some or all of these functions.

2   This chapter gives advice on appropriate levels of expertise, and on what training may be required, for those advising employers on hand-arm vibration risks and helping them comply with the Vibration Regulations.

3   Advice on suitable expertise and training courses for occupational physicians and nurses providing a health surveillance service for HAVS is given in Appendix 6.

Risk assessment and planning control actions

4   People who assess vibration risks and plan control actions on behalf of employers must be able to follow the guidance for employers in Parts 2 and 3 of this book. In general, they should have:

■   knowledge of the work processes in the industry concerned and familiarity with good practice;

■   an understanding of the purpose of risk assessment and what information needs to be obtained;

■   an understanding of how to obtain and interpret information on vibration risks, particularly manufacturers' declared emission values and any additional information about the likely vibration emitted by the equipment in use;

■   the ability to assess daily exposures from information on vibration magnitudes and exposure durations;

■   where required, competence in measurement of hand-arm vibration and interpretation of those measurements;

■   the ability to record their findings and decisions, and explain them to others; and

■   an understanding of their own limitations, whether of knowledge, experience or resources.

Training

5   Formal training is not a legal requirement. However, those offering a commercial service to duty-holders, and employers using their own personnel for this purpose, may wish to assure themselves that their staff have a suitable level of knowledge and expertise. This is particularly important if there is a requirement to measure vibration in the workplace.

6   A course covering the topics in Table 9 should provide a basis for dealing with most industrial vibration exposures, and recognising where more specialised expertise (for example in-depth knowledge of an industrial process or the

engineering application of vibration control) may be needed. Courses should ideally include a substantial practical element, and conclude with an assessment of the student's theoretical and practical competence.

7   Short training courses are available from a range of providers including universities, colleges, consultancies and other institutions. Some courses, organised through local training providers, are accredited by professional organisations including the following:

The Institute of Acoustics
77A St Peter's Street
St Albans
Herts
AL1 3BN

Tel: 01727 848195
www.ioa.org.uk

British Occupational Hygiene Society
Suite 2, Georgian House
Great Northern Road
Derby
DE1 1LT

Tel: 01332 298101
www.bohs.org

Table 9   Typical topics for training courses on hand-arm vibration risk management

Topic	*Important content*	*Useful additional content*
Legal requirements	Duties of employers to assess and manage risks from HAV: ■ the Control of Vibration at Work Regulations 2005; ■ the Reporting of Injuries, Diseases and Dangerous Occurrences Regulations 1995. Duties of manufacturers and suppliers of machinery: ■ the Supply of Machinery (Safety) Regulations 1992, as amended 1994.	■ The Health and Safety at Work etc. Act 1974. ■ The Management of Health and Safety at Work Regulations 1999. ■ The Provision and Use of Work Equipment Regulations 1998. ■ The Personal Protective Equipment at Work Regulations 1992. ■ The Workplace (Health, Safety and Welfare) Regulations 1992. ■ The Physical Agents (Vibration) Directive 2002/44/EC. ■ Harmonised European machinery safety standards.
Theory of vibration	Basic concepts: ■ displacement, velocity and acceleration; ■ root-mean-square time averaging; ■ vibration frequency.	Typical characteristics of sources of HAV: eg rotary, reciprocating and percussive tools.
Effects on health	Hand-arm vibration syndrome (HAVS): ■ neurological effects; ■ vascular effects; ■ musculoskeletal effects. Carpal tunnel syndrome.	Development of symptoms, dose-effect relationships. Clinical and laboratory techniques used in diagnosis of HAVS.

Topic	Important content	Useful additional content
Determining vibration magnitudes	Interpretation of manufacturers' declared emission values: ■ measurement conditions and standard methods; ■ appreciation of uncertainty. Principles of vibration measurement according to BS EN ISO 5349 Parts 1 and 2: ■ identifying the need for measurement in the workplace; ■ frequency weighting; ■ 3 axis vibration measurement techniques; ■ sampling strategies and appreciation of uncertainty; ■ recording and presenting vibration data.	■ Harmonised European vibration test codes Required if measurement is to be undertaken: ■ instrumentation and calibration; ■ accelerometers and mounting methods; ■ sources of measurement error; ■ practical experience.
Determining vibration exposures – calculation of $A(8)$	■ Understanding of daily vibration exposure $A(8)$ according to BS EN ISO 5349-1:2001. ■ Calculation of (partial) exposure from one tool or process. ■ Calculation of overall daily exposure from multiple vibration magnitudes and exposure times. ■ Recording and presenting the exposure results. ■ Comparison with the exposure action and limit values.	Use of exposure assessment tools provided by HSE: ■ exposure points system; ■ exposure calculator; ■ exposure ready-reckoner; ■ exposure nomogram.
Control of exposure	Elimination or reduction of vibration exposure by, eg: ■ substitution of new work process; ■ modification of process; ■ improving quality of manufactured product. Reduction of vibration exposure by, eg: ■ selecting lower vibration tools and equipment; ■ maintenance of equipment; ■ operator training. Reduction of daily exposure time by: ■ exposure points system; ■ job rotation; ■ permit-to-work systems; ■ more efficient tools and machinery.	Vibration sources - general principles of vibration generated by hand-held equipment and application of engineering principles to vibration control, eg: ■ auto-balancing for rotary machines; ■ vibration isolating handles; ■ energy absorption.

Topic	Important content	Useful additional content
Health surveillance	■ Simple health screening. ■ Selecting an occupational health provider. ■ Using health surveillance data to monitor control measures. ■ Management of affected workers.	Strategies and techniques for health surveillance.
Personal protective equipment	Use of clothing and gloves to keep warm to prevent blanching attacks etc. Anti-vibration gloves – their role, likely performance limitations and challenges in assessing their performance.	The standard for anti-vibration gloves, BS EN ISO 10819.
Guidance and literature	Introduction to sources of information, eg: ■ HSE publications; ■ Trade associations; ■ Trade Unions; ■ British, European and International standards.	
Note: This topic list is suggested as the basis for general courses. It may need to be amended to suit courses intended to train people for a particular range of tasks, eg those concerned with the management of HAV within a particular industry or company.		

Training syllabus for occupational health professionals

Faculty of Occupational Medicine of the Royal College of Physicians

Hand-arm vibration syndrome (HAVS)

This syllabus is intended to guide the training of occupational health care professionals in the requirements for health surveillance for a workforce exposed to hand-transmitted vibration, and in the diagnosis and management of an individual with HAVS. It is aimed at health professionals working in the UK occupational health setting, rather than in a medico-legal one.

Introduction

Background to HAVS

- Definition of HAVS

- Brief history of development of knowledge

- Faculty of Occupational Medicine reports 1993, 2004

- Prescribed disease

- RIDDOR reportable

- Vibration Regulations and HSE guidance

Epidemiology

- Number of people exposed in UK

- Prevalence of symptoms in UK

- Ubiquity of exposures in UK

- Examples of significantly exposed occupational groups

Overview of health surveillance (HSG61)

- Why health surveillance is needed

- Purpose of statutory health surveillance

- General criteria to be met for statutory health surveillance

- Indications for health surveillance, when it is likely to be needed, and also when it may not be appropriate

- Context of health surveillance, as part of the overall control measures

Legal

Relevant legislation and regulations

- Health and Safety at Work etc Act 1974

- Management of Health and Safety at Work Regulations 1999

- Control of Vibration at Work Regulations 2005

Overall requirements of the Regulations

- Assess the risk

- Avoid or reduce the risk

- Inform, train and consult workers

- Provide health surveillance

Risk assessment

- Factors to consider

- Role of vibration measurement

Exposure Action and Limit Values

- Definitions

- Units, and implications of time-weighted measurements

- What the values are

- Limitations, not 'safe' values

- Short-term exposures

Risk control

- Approaches to avoidance of exposure

- Risk-reduction measures

Information and training of workers

- Lay information sheet from Faculty of Occupational Medicine

- Role of health professionals in consultation with workers

Health surveillance; statutory requirements

- Purpose of health surveillance in HAVS

- Record-keeping

- Confidentiality and communication with management

- Provision of group data to management

Workplace vibration exposure

Exposures and their measurement and reporting

- Practicalities of vibration measurement

- Terminology relating to vibration/acceleration (see legal section)

- Accelerometers

- Single axis versus tri axial measurements

Relevant International/British Standards

- ISO 5349

- Supply of Machinery (Safety) Regulations and vibration declaration

- Considerations relating to standard testing of vibration emissions

Illustrations of different types of tool causing hand-transmitted vibration

- Hand-held tools

- Hand-fed machinery

- Hand-guided machinery

- Examples of vibration measurements for different tools, including beneficial effects of maintenance

Ergonomics of tool use

- Importance of grip strength/feed force as a factor in disease

- Weight of tools and how to reduce/overcome this

- Postural aspects of tool use

- Manual handling aspects of jobs

Aetiology

Exposure-response relationship

- The exposure response model in BS 6842 and the effects of duration of exposure and acceleration magnitude

- The ISO exposure response model, and the background to its derivation

- Limitations of the ISO model

- Other general information on exposure response contained in the Annexes to ISO

- Lack of detailed information on exposure-response relationship for the sensorineural and musculoskeletal components of HAVS

Latency

- The concept of latency in relation to the onset of the vascular component

- The relationship between vibration magnitude and latent period for vascular effects, with examples

Pathophysiology

Vascular component

- Physiology of control of peripheral circulation

- Local versus central hypothesis

- Evidence of harm: larger vessels and capillaries

- Changes in blood components

Neurological

- Skin receptor types

- Innervation of receptors

- Evidence of local damage to nerve fibres

- Effects of pressure on larger nerve trunks

- Carpal tunnel syndrome, ulnar nerve damage at the wrist

- Differences between 'classical' entrapment carpal tunnel and carpal tunnel syndrome associated with HAVS

Musculoskeletal component

- Physiological effects of vibration on muscle

- Vibration tonic reflex

- Reduction in grip strength

- Aetiology, damage to nerve or muscle?

Skeletal system

- Bony outgrowths, bone vacuoles, osteoarthritis

- Evidence of reversibility, progress and prognosis

Health effects of hand-transmitted vibration

Vascular: secondary Raynaud's phenomena

- Blanching of finger tips

- Progression of symptoms with continuing exposure

- Phases of a 'typical' episode of vasospasm

- Triggers for vasospasm

Sensorineural including nerve entrapment

- Initial onset often neurological

- Altered thermal sensitivity

- Effects on dexterity

Musculoskeletal symptoms

- Impaired grip strength

- Upper limb pain

- Osteoarthritis

Other conditions

- Dupuytren's disease, sensorineural hearing loss

- Overall impact of symptoms on functional ability and work/social life

Differential diagnosis

Prevalence of symptoms in non-exposed population

- Vascular: Primary Raynaud's and Secondary Raynaud's disease including connective tissue disease, eg scleroderma, trauma, occlusive vascular disease and hypersensitivity

- Neurological: Carpal tunnel syndrome, diabetes mellitus etc

- Other: Hypothenar hammer syndrome, thoracic outlet syndrome etc

Classification

- General uses of classification

- Consistency

- Longitudinal follow up

- Decisions on deployment

- Clinical audit

- Research

Stockholm Workshop Scale

- Vascular: Limitations of the scale

- Neurological: Limitations of the scale

The scales in practice

- Pen pictures of typical symptoms at stages 2 and 3, Vascular and Neurological

- Repeatability and agreement between observers

Other approaches

- Griffin scoring

Details of health surveillance programme

Setting up the programme

- Overview of the programme

- Roles of the various parties

- Training of the various parties

- Communication with employer and workers, information and education for workers

- Health records

- Pitfalls

Pre-employment assessment: evidence of pre-existing vulnerability

Level 1 questionnaire, possible individual risk factors

Screening assessment, including frequency of assessment

Level 2 short questionnaire (responsible person)

Level 3 occupational health nurse (qualified person)

Level 4 occupational physician (medical officer)

Referral methods

Level 5 standardised testing

Clinical assessment

- Value of information recorded at lower tiers

Approach to the patient

- Overview of symptoms

- Free text record of symptoms

- Questioning from standardised questionnaire

- The sections in the questionnaire

Clinical examination

- Inspection

- Tests

Standardised tests

- Vascular

- Neurological

- Musculoskeletal

How to synthesise the information obtained to reach an overall classification

Management of cases of HAVS

Advice to employees and employers, including confidentiality issues

Prognosis and reversibility

- Available options for therapeutic interventions

- Measures to reduce ongoing vibration exposure

- General advice on reducing the impact of the condition, eg keeping warm avoiding smoking, noise exposure

- Accepted guidance on deployment action at Stage 2 and Stage 3

- Special consideration for cases with rapid progression or other individual factors

- Individual functional assessment, disability and judging fitness for work, including safety issues

- Possible application of Disability Discrimination Act?

Medico-legal and regulatory considerations

- Reporting under RIDDOR with consent

- Prescribed disease and industrial injuries benefit issues

- Compensation/civil claim

COMPETENCIES

The following will be required by candidates:

SUBJECT AREA	KNOWLEDGE Have sufficient knowledge of:	SKILL	UNDERSTANDING	COMPETENCY
ASSESSMENT OF EXPOSURE	The regulatory and legal framework Workers, workforces, tools and processes with significant exposure to hand-transmitted vibration and at increased risk of HAVS Terminology of acceleration and vibration measurement Practicalities of vibration measurement	Apply this knowledge to a specific individual and specific workforce Interpret results from formal measurements of vibration exposure in light of the Regulations	Understand the limitations of current models of the exposure-response relationship, and the consequent limitations of relying entirely on adherence to an exposure limit as the sole control measure	Possess the ability to assess the exposure to hand-transmitted vibration in a specific workforce Provide appropriate advice regarding this exposure, including any requirement for health surveillance, in line with the Regulations
HEALTH SURVEILLANCE	General requirements and criteria for health surveillance, including ethical and confidentiality considerations Specific requirements and criteria for health surveillance in the context of HAVS The different levels of health surveillance	Determine which workers should undergo health surveillance, which level of health surveillance is appropriate, how frequently this should be performed and by whom	Appreciate the role of health surveillance as part of a package which will help employers to comply with all requirements of the Regulations Understand how to to instigate an appropriate health surveillance programme, and how to avoid the common pitfalls	Appropriately advise when health surveillance is required, when it may not be required, and what is involved Communicate this advice in appropriate language to employers and employees
ASSESSMENT OF THE INDIVIDUAL	The anatomy and physiology of the upper limb, including the physiology of the control of peripheral circulation Diseases and clinical conditions associated with hand-transmitted vibration The aetiology and pathophysiology of the clinical conditions comprising HAVS The differential diagnosis and approximate prevalence of these conditions in the working population	Have sufficient clinical skills to: (a) take and record a relevant medical history from an individual; in particular to include other conditions or medications which may mimic HAVS; (b) take and record a complete chronological work history; in particular to obtain an estimate of the duration and extent of vibration exposure or exposure to neurotoxic agents; (c) determine any non-occupational vibration exposure;	Appreciate the gaps in our knowledge and understanding of the clinical aspects of HAVS, and in particular of: (a) the reliance on the history obtained in making a diagnosis and the absence of any diagnostic test or combination of tests; (b) limitations of the standardised tests; (c) limitations of the Stockholm Workshop scale;	Perform a suitable clinical assessment of an individual; including a medical and occupational history, clinical examination and consideration for the requirements for and results of standardised tests. This process should be sufficient to make a diagnosis or differential diagnosis, and where necessary to apply a Stockholm grading

SUBJECT AREA	KNOWLEDGE Have sufficient knowledge of:	SKILL	UNDERSTANDING	COMPETENCY
ASSESSMENT OF THE INDIVIDUAL *Cont...*	The Stockholm Workshop scale and other grading systems	(d) describe the impairment, disability and handicap arising from these medical disorders, in particular their effect on a person's ability to work and on access to daily living and leisure activities; (e) perform an appropriate clinical examination, including relevant office tests; (f) determine when standardised tests are indicated, and interpret the results of these; (g) formulate a diagnosis and differential diagnosis; where appropriate apply a grading according to the Stockholm Workshop scale.		
PROVISION OF ADVICE TO INDIVIDUAL AND TO MANAGEMENT	The prognosis, benefits of exposure reduction, avoidance of precipitants and contributory factors Treatment options and benefits Issues of confidentiality and the provision of group data to the employer The recommendations of expert groups for management or cessation of exposure at particular Stockholm stages Medico-legal, financial and regulatory requirements including RIDDOR reporting, industrial injuries benefits and compensation	Explain specialist terms and recommendations to lay persons (employee and employer) Interpret recommendations of expert groups for management at particular Stockholm stages in light of individual factors and circumstances	Understand the limitations of rigid adherence to the management of the individual based only upon Stockholm staging; appreciate circumstances to deviate from this Appreciate the implications of any advice to the individual, employer and wider community	Provide suitable, comprehensible advice to the individual and employer to enable all parties to make informed decisions

Guidance for machinery manufacturers on a suggested approach to warning of residual risk from vibration

1   Machinery manufacturers and suppliers have a duty to provide information to their customers to help protect against residual risks from HAV. Where the declared vibration emission (measured using the appropriate test code) is not sufficiently representative of the likely vibration magnitudes to warn of risk, more information is required. The example below suggests how a manufacturer might present this information in the instruction manual supplied with the machine (a chipping hammer in this fictitious example).

Risk of hand-arm vibration injury

Example

Vibration emission

Chipping hammer, make ABC, type 123, model 45, when operated in accordance with these instructions and tested in accordance with EN 28662-2:1994 results in the following vibration emission declared in accordance with EN 12096:1996.

Measured vibration emission value	*a*	8.0 m/s²
Uncertainty	*K*	2.3 m/s²

These values are suitable for comparison with the vibration emission levels of other tools that have been obtained using the same test method.

Note: These data represent the vibration in the z-axis on the main handle. The z-axis is not always the direction of greatest vibration on the main handle when the tool is in use and much higher vibration magnitudes occur at the other hand position on the main body of the tool. Furthermore, vibration exposure assessments are based not on vibration in a single direction, but on the 'vibration total value' which is a greater value obtained from the x-, y- and z-axis values.

This tool may cause hand-arm vibration syndrome if its use is not adequately managed.

The vibration emission from chipping hammers varies greatly with the task, with the operator's grip and the feed force. We believe that normal intended use of the tool will usually produce vibration emissions at the hand position on the body of the tool that vary between 15 and 20 m/s² (vibration total value) depending on the details of the task but emissions outside this range may occur for some applications. A figure of 18 m/s² is probably a useful typical emission value, say, for estimating the likely average exposures (and hence risk) in accordance with EN ISO 5349-1:2001 of tool users performing a wide range of tasks within the intended use of the tool.

We point out that application of the tool to a sole specialist task may produce a different average emission, and in such cases we recommend a specific evaluation of the vibration emission, but we would expect the average to fall between 15 and 20 m/s².

Recommended measures to reduce the risk of hand-arm vibration syndrome

Restricting exposure time

The tool should not be used by an individual regularly for more than 10 minutes (hands-on power-on) in any one day; longer exposure times are likely to exceed the Control of Vibration at Work Regulations exposure action value for hand-arm vibration. The tool should never be used for more than 40 minutes in any one day as this is likely to exceed the exposure limit value. The duration of use should be further reduced if the individual is exposed to hand-arm vibration from other sources.

Correct use and maintenance

The vibration emission is closely linked to the operating pressure in the air supply. You should ensure that the pressure is set in accordance with our recommendations to assure optimum efficiency with minimised vibration exposure.

The transmission of vibration to the user is reduced by the inclusion of components A and B [an exploded diagram might be used to identify components A and B]. The condition of these components should be checked and they should be replaced every *n* months during routine maintenance and earlier if they show signs of wear or age.

Health surveillance

We recommend a programme of health surveillance to detect early symptoms of vibration injury so that management procedures can be modified to help prevent significant handicap.

Personal protective equipment

We are not aware of any personal protective equipment (PPE) that provides protection against vibration injury by attenuating the vibration emissions of this tool. We recommend a sufficient supply of clothing (including gloves) to enable the operator to remain warm and dry and maintain good blood circulation in fingers etc.

2   Where a tool is designed for a well-defined use it is sometimes helpful to describe the recommended maximum daily use in terms of work done, rather than simply the exposure duration. This is because a less powerful or less efficient machine, although producing less vibration, may give an overall greater vibration exposure for a given task, due to the increased time it takes to do the job. For example, the manufacturer could advise that a drilling machine can be used to drill a certain number of holes (of known size in a known material) before the exposure action or limit value is likely to be reached. The following example shows how the manufacturer of a hammer drill might present this information.

Recommended measures to reduce the risk of hand-arm vibration syndrome

Limiting exposure time

The tool should not be used by any individual regularly for more than about 20 minutes (hands-on power-on) in any one day; a longer exposure time is likely to exceed the exposure action value for hand-arm vibration. The tool should never be operated by any individual for more than about 1 hour 20 minutes in any one day as this is likely to exceed the legal exposure limit value. The duration of use should be further reduced if the individual is also exposed to hand-arm vibration from other sources on the same day.

Tests have shown that this tool is capable of performing the following number of holes in concrete (40 N/m² compressive strength) before the operator reaches the exposure action and limit values:

To exposure action value: 50-60 holes 100 mm deep or equivalent

To exposure limit value: 200-230 holes 100 mm deep or equivalent

These figures apply to a tool in good condition, with a sharp insert (type XYZ, diameter 5-14 mm), operated in accordance with these instructions. Drill diameters up to 20 mm can be used with this machine, but the vibration emissions will be greater and the working time/number of holes drilled should be restricted accordingly.

References

1   *Whole-body vibration. The Control of Vibration at Work Regulations 2005. Guidance on Regulations* L141 HSE Books 2005 ISBN 0 7176 6126 1 (Due to be published in late 2005)

2   *Control the risks from hand-arm vibration: Advice for employers on the Control of Vibration at Work Regulations 2005* Leaflet INDG175(rev2) HSE Books 2005 (single copy free or priced packs of 10 ISBN 0 7176 6117 2)

3   *Hand-arm vibration: Advice for employees* Pocket card INDG296(rev1) HSE Books 2005 (single copy free or priced packs of 25 ISBN 0 7176 6118 0)

4   *Managing health and safety in construction: Construction (Design and Management) Regulations 1994. Approved Code of Practice and guidance* HSG224 HSE Books 2001 ISBN 0 7176 2139 1

5   *The Health and Safety (Training for Employment) Regulations 1990* SI 1990/1380 The Stationery Office 1990 ISBN 0 11 004380 4

6   *Machinery. Guidance notes on UK Regulations. Guidance on the Supply of Machinery (Safety) Regulations 1992 as amended by the Supply of Machinery (Safety) (Amendment) Regulations 1994* URN 95/650 Department of Trade and Industry 1995 (Available from the DTI Publications Orderline: 0845 015 0010)

7   *Management of health and safety at work. Management of Health and Safety at Work Regulations 1999. Approved Code of Practice and guidance* L21 (Second edition) HSE Books 2000 ISBN 0 7176 2488 9

8   *Safety representatives and safety committees* L87 (Third edition) HSE Books 1996 ISBN 0 7176 1220 1

9   *A guide to the Offshore Installations (Safety Representatives and Safety Committees) Regulations 1989. Guidance on Regulations* L110 (Second edition) HSE Books 1998 ISBN 0 7176 1549 9

10   *A guide to the Health and Safety (Consultation with Employees) Regulations 1996. Guidance on Regulations* L95 HSE Books 1996 ISBN 0 7176 1234 1

11   *A guide to the Reporting of Injuries, Diseases and Dangerous Occurrences Regulations 1995* L73 (Second edition) HSE Books 1999 ISBN 0 7176 2431 5

12   *Safe use of work equipment. Provision and Use of Work Equipment Regulations 1998. Approved Code of Practice and guidance* L22 (Second edition) HSE Books 1998 ISBN 0 7176 1626 6

13   *Workplace health, safety and welfare. Workplace (Health, Safety and Welfare) Regulations 1992. Approved Code of Practice* L24 HSE Books 1992 ISBN 0 7176 0413 6

14   *Need help on health and safety? Guidance for employers on when and how to get advice on health and safety* Leaflet INDG322 HSE Books 2000 (single copy free or priced packs of 10 ISBN 0 7176 1790 4)

15   BS EN 12096:1997 *Mechanical vibration. Declaration and verification of vibration emission values*

16   BS EN ISO 20643:2005 *Mechanical vibration. Hand-held and hand-guided machinery. Principles for evaluation of vibration emission*

17   BS EN ISO 5349-1:2001 *Mechanical vibration. Measurement and evaluation of human exposure to hand-transmitted vibration. General requirements*

18   *Health surveillance at work* HSG61 (Second edition) HSE Books 1999 ISBN 0 7176 1705 X

19   BS EN ISO 5349-2:2002 *Mechanical vibration. Measurement and assessment of human exposure to hand-transmitted vibration. Practical guidance for measurement at the workplace*

20   BS EN ISO 8041:2005 *Human response to vibration. Measuring instrumentation*

21   BS EN ISO 10819:1997 *Mechanical vibration and shock. Hand-arm vibration. Method for the measurement and evaluation of the vibration transmissibility of gloves at the palm of the hand* (under revision in 2005)

22   *Personal Protective Equipment at Work (Second edition). Personal Protective Equipment at Work Regulations 1992 (as amended). Guidance on Regulations* L25 HSE Books 2005 ISBN 0 7176 6139 3

23   *Standardised diagnostic methods for assessing components of the hand-arm vibration syndrome* (Lindsell and Griffin) CRR197 HSE Books 1998 ISBN 0 7176 1640 1

24   Griffin MJ *The effects of vibration on health* (ISVR Memorandum 632) Institute of Sound and Vibration Research, University of Southampton, 1982

25   Lawson IJ and McGeoch KL 'A medical assessment procedure for a large number of medico-legal compensation claims for hand-arm vibration syndrome' *Occupational Medicine* 2003 **53** 302-308

Further reading

This list does not include those publications or Standards already mentioned in the 'References' section.

HSE guidance

Hard to handle: Hand-arm vibration – managing the risk Video HSE Books 1998 ISBN 0 7176 1881 1

Use of contractors: A joint responsibility Leaflet INDG368 HSE Books 2002 (single copy free or priced packs of 10 ISBN 0 7176 2566 4)

Hazards associated with foundry processes: Hand-arm vibration - the current picture Foundries Information Sheet FNIS8 HSE 1996 Web only version available at http://www.hse.gov.uk/pubns/founindx.htm

Hazards associated with foundry processes: Hand-arm vibration - assessing the need for action Foundries Information Sheet FNIS10 HSE 1999 Web only version available at http://www.hse.gov.uk/pubns/founindx.htm

Hand-arm vibration in foundries: Furnace and ladle relining operations Foundries Information Sheet FNIS11 HSE 2002 Web only version available at http://www.hse.gov.uk/pubns/founindx.htm

A purchasing policy for vibration-reduced tools in foundries Foundries Information Sheet FNIS12 HSE 2002 Web only version available at http://www.hse.gov.uk/pubns/founindx.htm

HSE research reports (available free at www.hse.gov.uk/research/publish.htm)

Bomel Ltd *Improving health and safety in construction: Phase 2 Depth and breadth. Volume 4 Hand Arm Vibration Syndrome. Underlying causes and risk control in the construction industry* RR114 HSE Books 2003 ISBN 0 7176 2219 3

Griffin MJ & Lindsell CJ *Cold provocation tests for the diagnosis of vibration-induced white finger: Standardisation and repeatability* CRR173 HSE Books 1998 ISBN 0 7176 1574 X

Mitchell RH et al *Implications of the Physical Agents (Vibration) Directive for SMEs* RR267 HSE Books 2004 ISBN 0 7176 2893 0

Paddan GS & Griffin MJ *Standard tests for the vibration transmissibility of gloves* CRR249 HSE Books 1999 ISBN 0 7176 1719 X

Paddan GS et al *Hand-transmitted vibration: Evaluation of some common sources of exposure in Great Britain* CRR234 HSE Books 1999 ISBN 0 7176 2480 3

Palmer KT et al *Hand-transmitted vibration: Occupational exposures and their health effects in Great Britain* CRR232 HSE Books 1999 ISBN 0 7176 2476 5

Stayner RM *European grinder vibration test code: A critical review* CRR135 HSE Books 1997 ISBN 0 7176 1384 4

Stayner RM *Grinder characteristics and their effects on hand-arm vibration* CRR115 HSE Books 1996 ISBN 0 7176 1265 1

Stayner RM *Isolation and auto-balancing techniques for portable machines* RR078 HSE Books 2003 ISBN 0 7176 2674 1

Other publications

Gemne G et al 'The Stockholm workshop scale for the classification of cold-induced Raynaud's phenomenon in the hand-arm vibration syndrome' *Scandinavian Journal of Work, Environment and Health* 1987 13(4), 275-6

Griffin MJ *Handbook of human vibration* Academic Press 1990 ISBN 0 12 303040 4

Mason H and Poole K *Clinical testing and management of individuals exposed to hand-transmitted vibration. An evidence review* Faculty of Occupational Medicine of the Royal College of Physicians 2004 ISBN 1 86016 203 7

'Stockholm Workshop 86: Symptomatology and diagnostic methods in the hand-arm vibration syndrome' *Scandinavian Journal of Work Environment and Health* 4 (special issue), 1987, 271-388

Eighth International Conference on Hand-Arm Vibration, 9-12 June 1998, Umeå, Sweden. Proceedings

Ninth International Conference on Hand-Arm Vibration, 5-8 June 2001, Nancy, France. Proceedings

Tenth International Conference on Hand-Arm Vibration, 7-11 June 2004, Las Vegas, USA. Proceedings (awaiting publication, 2005)

Machinery safety standards and vibration emission test codes

BS EN 792 series *Hand-held non-electric power tools – Safety requirements* (These standards refer to BS EN 28662/BS EN ISO 8662 series for vibration testing.)

BS EN 28662/BS EN ISO 8662 series *Hand-held portable power tools. Measurement of vibrations at the handle* (Test codes for specific families of power tools, especially pneumatic tools. Subject to a programme of revision to reflect requirements of BS EN ISO 20643:2005.)

BS EN 60745 series. *Hand-held motor-operated electric tools. Safety* (General safety standards for specific families of electric power tools. Supersedes the BS EN 50144 series of standards.)

BS EN 1454:1997 *Portable hand-held internal combustion cutting-off machines. Safety*

BS EN 12418:2000 *Masonry and stone cutting off machines for job site. Safety*

BS EN 709:1997 *Agricultural and forestry machinery. Pedestrian controlled tractors with mounted rotary cultivators, motor hoes, motor hoes with drive wheels. Safety*

BS EN 745:1999 *Agricultural machinery. Rotary mowers and flail mowers. Safety*

BS EN ISO 11681-1:2004 *Machinery for forestry. Portable chainsaws. Safety requirements and testing. Chainsaws for forest service*

BS EN 12733:2001 *Agricultural and forestry machinery. Pedestrian controlled motor mowers. Safety*

BS EN ISO 22867:2004 *Forestry machinery. Vibration test code for portable hand-held machines with internal combustion engine. Vibration at the handles*

BS EN 774:1996 *Garden equipment. Hand-held integrally powered hedge trimmers. Safety*

BS EN 786:1996 (amended 2001) *Garden equipment. Electrically powered walk-behind and lawn edge trimmers. Mechanical safety*

BS EN 836:1997 *Garden equipment. Powered lawnmowers. Safety*

Further information

HSE priced and free publications are available by mail order from HSE Books, PO Box 1999, Sudbury, Suffolk CO10 2WA Tel: 01787 881165 Fax: 01787 313995 Website: www.hsebooks.co.uk (HSE priced publications are also available from bookshops and free leaflets can be downloaded from HSE's website: www.hse.gov.uk.)

British Standards are available from BSI Customer Services, 389 Chiswick High Road, London W4 4AL Tel: 020 8996 9001 Fax: 020 8996 7001 e-mail: cservices@bsi-global.com Website: www.bsi-global.com

The Stationery Office publications are available from The Stationery Office, PO Box 29, Norwich NR3 1GN Tel: 0870 600 5522 Fax: 0870 600 5533 e-mail: customer.services@tso.co.uk Website: www.tso.co.uk (They are also available from bookshops.)

For information about health and safety ring HSE's Infoline Tel: 0845 345 0055 Fax: 0845 408 9566 Textphone: 0845 408 9577 e-mail: hseinfoline@natbrit.com or write to HSE Information Services, Caerphilly Business Park, Caerphilly CF83 3GG.

Printed and published by the Health and Safety Executive   C100   09/05